Recent Research in Psychology

J.D. Fisher   R.C. Silver
J.M. Chinsky   B. Goff   Y. Klar

Evaluating a Large Group Awareness Training

A Longitudinal Study of Psychosocial Effects

Springer-Verlag
New York Berlin Heidelberg
London Paris Toyko Hong Kong

Jeffrey D. Fisher, PhD, Department of Psychology, University of Connecticut, Storrs, Connecticut 06269-1020, USA

Roxane Cohen Silver, PhD, Program in Social Ecology, University of California, Irvine, Irvine, California 92717, USA

Jack M. Chinsky, PhD, Department of Psychology, University of Connecticut, Storrs, Connecticut 06269-1020, USA

Barry Goff, PhD, Department of Psychology, University of Connecticut, Storrs, Connecticut 06269-1020, USA

Yechiel Klar, PhD, Department of Psychology, University of Connecticut, Storrs, Connecticut 06269-1020, USA

Library of Congress Cataloging-in-Publication Data
Evaluating a large group awareness training : a longitudinal study of
  psychosocial effects / J.D. Fisher . . . [et al.], authors.
      p.   cm. — (Recent research in psychology)
   Includes bibliographical references.
   ISBN 0-387-97320-6. — ISBN 3-540-97320-6
   1. Group relations training — Longitudinal studies.   2. Group
relations training — Evaluation.   I. Fisher, Jeffrey D., 1949-   .
II. Series.
   HM134.E93   1990
   302′.14 — dc20   90-36700

Printed on acid-free paper.

Camera-ready copy provided by the authors.
Printed and bound by Edwards Brothers, Inc., Ann Arbor, Michigan.
Printed in the United States of America.

9 8 7 6 5 4 3 2 1

ISBN 0-387-97320-6 Springer-Verlag New York Berlin Heidelberg
ISBN 3-540-97320-6 Springer-Verlag Berlin Heidelberg New York

Dedication

In memory of Jack Mantos:

For his tireless support of this research and for giving us the complete freedom to perform it. Although he might not have agreed with all our findings, he would have no doubt wanted them to serve as the impetus for continued methodologically rigorous research in this area.

Acknowledgements

This research was supported by mixed sources grant number 1171-000-11-00215-14-626 to the University of Connecticut. We thank Werner Erhard and Associates who permitted the researchers access to the Forum subject population, and under whose auspices the funds for conducting this study were provided. This program of research was conducted under a formal agreement between Werner Erhard and Associates and the researchers, dated May 6, 1985, guaranteeing the researchers complete independence in every phase of the project. For a copy of the agreement with the University of Connecticut, see Appendix B. A similar agreement was also signed with the University of Waterloo. We also wish to express our appreciation to Thomas Malloy for his statistical consultation. In addition, Ellen Amore, Lis Cade, Rena Epstein, Robert Green, Pamela Kerouack, Diane Kimble, Donald Meichenbaum, Richard Mendola, Amy Reichard, Lisa Ross, Ann Sharp, Patty Sivo, Carol Valone, and Cyndi Zagieboylo are acknowledged for the important role they played in various phases of the research.

A condensed version of some of the material contained in this volume appeared in *Journal of Consulting and Clinical Psychology* (Fisher, Silver, Chinsky, Goff, Klar, & Zagieboylo, 1989). We thank the American Psychological Association for granting us permission to reprint the relevant material.

This research was conducted while Roxane Cohen Silver was on the faculty of the University of Waterloo, Canada. Barry Goff is now with the Human Interface Group, Hartford, Connecticut, and Yechiel Klar is at the Department of Psychology, University of Kansas.

The research reported in this volume was awarded the American Psychological Association, Division 13, National Psychological Consultants to Management Award, August 13, 1989.

Contents

Chapter I
Introduction

Large Group Awareness Training: An Historical Context

Groups associated with the human potential movement have been a controversial feature of American life during the last three decades. In the 1950's and 1960's, the movement was dominated by various types of small groups (SGs), which included sensitivity training groups, encounter groups, as well as several others (see Lieberman, Yalom, & Miles, 1973). Some people viewed SGs as an effective means for attaining personal and organizational growth, and Carl Rogers, one of the founders of this movement, labeled small groups as "the most rapidly spreading social invention of the century, and probably the most potent" (Rogers, 1970). In contrast, others attacked SGs as "the most extreme exhibition thus far of man's talent for reducing, distorting, evading, and vulgarizing his own reality" (Koch, 1973, p. 639). Nevertheless, SGs generally became an accepted tool for personal development and were incorporated into university curricula and managerial training programs.

During the 1970's the prevalence and appeal of SGs declined (cf. Back, 1978), and at about the same time, large group awareness training programs (LGATs) appeared.[1] LGATs are offered to the general public by profit-making organizations and examine philosophical, psychological and ethical issues concerning personal effectiveness, decision-making, personal responsibility and commitment. After addressing these topics, participants are encouraged to apply their recently attained insights to their lives. This is assumed not only to help them resolve any problems they might have, but also to intensify perception and experience so that productivity is increased and participants feel more "alive." (For more detailed discussions, see Emery, 1977; Erhard & Gioscia, 1977.)

The Erhard Seminars Training (*est*) was the first LGAT to emerge during the early 1970's. It was followed by other groups such as Lifespring, Actualizations, Insight, Relationships, and more recently, the Forum, the successor to *est*. The number of participants in these groups is substantial. For example, over 480,000 people participated in *est* between 1971 and 1985 (Werner Erhard & Associates,

---

[1]Psychologists have often classified LGATs as a generic group (cf. Finkelstein, Wenegrat, & Yalom, 1982). While this classification does have considerable heuristic value and will be used throughout the present volume, it must be kept in mind that each of these interventions are unique.

1989), 300,000 people have taken part in the Lifespring basic training to date (Lifespring, 1989), and over 120,000 people have attended the Forum since its introduction in 1985 (Werner Erhard & Associates, 1989).

From a procedural perspective, LGAT groups are generally quite similar (see descriptions in Bry, 1976; Haaken & Adams, 1983; Winstow, 1986). In the typical program, individuals pay significant sums of money to participate in a training. Training groups range in size from a few dozen to several hundred people, who are gathered in a large room for approximately 12 hours a day for four or five days. The room is usually arranged so that participants are seated facing a podium, where the group leader stands. Following lectures given by the leader, participants discuss issues, ask questions, and make comments on LGAT themes. Structured exercises such as guided imagery and sharing of experiences in dyads or small groups are also part of the program. However, unlike SG training, there is relatively little face-to-face interaction among LGAT participants during the sessions, although they are encouraged to applaud the disclosures made by others and to discuss LGAT themes in smaller groups during breaks.

Some LGATs, notably *est*, were reported to have had more extreme procedures, which included limiting the participants' sleep time, their opportunities to use the bathrooms during the sessions, and their consumption of food, beverages, and cigarettes. In particular, the leaders' approaches were considered authoritarian and their routine use of derogatory comments directed toward the participants was considered by some to be unduly rigid (cf. Fenwick, 1976; Rome, 1977). However, these procedures are not standard in all LGAT programs.

After the training is completed, many LGAT organizations promote continued involvement. The graduates are encouraged to "share" their LGAT experiences with friends and family and to volunteer for administrative duties in its service. Additionally, LGAT graduates are expected to introduce the LGAT to members of their social network and to encourage their participation. Some organizations also sponsor community and volunteer activities, which the participants are encouraged to join.[2]

Although supporters of LGATs consider them to be vehicles for personal growth and community involvement, many people are concerned about the purposes and effects of these organizations. Some fear that they may be harmful to participants. Others take issue with the methods used, and still others are critical of the fact that LGATs seem to emphasize participants' recruiting friends and relatives into this often costly activity. These concerns, as well as other issues, have generated a great deal of controversy.

---

[2]For example, the Forum is aligned with charitable organizations such as The Hunger Project, The Breakthrough Foundation, The Holiday Project, and The Educational Network (Werner Erhard & Associates, 1985). Lifespring is associated with Pathway to Peace (Lifespring, 1987).

The Controversy Surrounding LGATs

Since their initiation, LGATs have attracted much attention from the general public. There have been several documentaries on these interventions, a considerable amount of news coverage, and dozens of books have been written on the subject (e.g., Bartley, 1978; Bry, 1976; Emery, 1977; Fenwick, 1976; Rhinehart, 1976; Rosen, 1977; Tipton, 1982; Winstow, 1986). Some of these have attempted to understand, others to glorify, and still others to denounce LGATs. Overall, the sources of information about LGATs are frequently contradictory, and there is a great deal of unresolved controversy between LGAT advocates and antagonists.

This controversy is especially pronounced in the mental health field, and although many of the issues are similar to the controversies of more than 20 years ago surrounding SGs, the responses to LGATs are much stronger and more polarized. The differences between the two movements may explain the more extreme reactions to LGATs. First, the SG movement grew from within the field of psychology, as well as related scientific disciplines, and was associated with well-respected psychologists such as Kurt Lewin, Abraham Maslow, Rollo May, and Carl Rogers. LGATs, on the other hand, were started by commercial groups outside the mental health community. In general, their founders were people with no recognized professional or academic background, and these individuals were at times perceived as having made a great deal of money from the groups they introduced. In addition, no written theory provides a rationale for LGATs, they are typically run by non-psychologists, and the participants are sometimes asked not to disclose the specific content of LGAT sessions. LGATs also reflect a more drastic change from the traditional approach to mental health, which usually involves a one-on-one relationship. Because LGATs involve hundreds of people at a session being influenced by one leader, some also believe that LGATs constitute a potentially dangerous form of social influence (Cinnamon & Farson, 1979; Rome, 1977).

Three related issues are at the center of the LGAT controversy. The first concerns the specific techniques used in LGAT. The second concerns whether or not LGAT should be considered a form of psychotherapy. The third and most important issue concerns whether LGATs are beneficial or detrimental to participants. Each of these issues has provoked heated discussions, but little behavioral research has been conducted to substantiate the opposing views.

LGAT Techniques

Since the initiation of LGATs, critics have been concerned about what they perceive to be the use of manipulative and authoritarian techniques by the leaders; the term "brainwashing" has been even been used in this context (cf. Brewer,

1975; Rome, 1977). Rogers, one of the leaders of the SG movement, commented on LGATs, saying that "...their goals are not too bad, actually, but their means are horrendously authoritarian. I feel that they have lost completely the distinction between means and goals" (cited in Conway & Siegelman, 1978, p. 222). However, others regard the authoritarian techniques as facilitating favorable outcomes and see them as implemented only to achieve positive results (see, e.g., Spiegel, 1983). One of the founders of *est* described its technique as a "communication in a context of compassion" (Erhard & Gioscia, 1978).

Is LGAT a Form of Psychotherapy?

Another issue at the center of the controversy surrounding LGATs is whether or not they should be viewed as a form of psychotherapy. Some psychologists and mental health professionals do consider the groups to be legitimate therapy, to contain therapeutic elements, or to be an adjunct to therapy (Berger, 1977; Paul & Paul, 1978; Simon, 1978). For example, Baer and Stolz (1978) described the ways in which LGATs make use of behavior modification techniques, and Yalom (1980) described the similarity between LGATs and existential group therapies. Others have compared LGATs to transactional analysis (Klein, 1983) or family therapy (Efran, Lukens, & Lukens, 1986; Simon, 1986). In addition, of a group of mental health professionals who were themselves *est* graduates, most said they would recommend it to clients and make use of it in their professional work (*est*, 1977).

However, many members of the mental health community believe that LGATs are practicing illegitimate psychotherapy (e.g., Fenwick, 1976; Kilbourne & Richardson, 1984), and in one case in 1975, the State Board of Practicing Psychologists in Hawaii ruled that *est* was practicing psychology without a license (Weiss, 1977). LGAT organizers define the groups not as therapy but as an educational or philosophical experience, and LGAT participants are required to affirm that they are aware that the LGAT is neither designed nor intended as therapy. Hamsher (1976), in comparing *est* to psychotherapy, emphasized that they are two distinct experiences. Therapy, he claims, is based on the tacit agreement that the client needs some improvement in a certain area and that the therapist can provide assistance toward this goal. He contrasts this position with the one held by *est*, which states that the participants are fine the way they are (Hamsher, 1976). Nevertheless, it is likely that many people with problems may enroll in LGATs expecting help, and although LGATs may not explicitly state that their purpose is therapeutic, receiving help for problems may be an implicit recruiting message. Overall, the issue of whether or not LGATs are a form of psychotherapy is a complex philosophical one that will be difficult to resolve, since even the term "psychotherapy" cannot be defined with certainty (cf. Frank, 1961, 1985; Friedman, 1976; Grinker, 1956).

Are LGATs Detrimental or Beneficial to Mental Health?

Probably the most critical issue in the controversy surrounding LGATs concerns whether they are harmful or beneficial to clients. In fact, the debates surrounding this issue are no less polarized than those concerned with the former questions. LGAT protagonists cite numerous testimonials of positive and sometimes even dramatic outcomes, and those who responded to a newsletter survey sent to *est* graduates indicated that their LGAT participation was more "useful to their quality of life" (on average) than such life domains as education, employment, recreation, art, religion, or government. Moreover, LGAT participation was considered to be only slightly less "useful to quality of life" than family and relationships (*est*, 1980). (It should be noted, however, that this study was flawed by self-selection and other serious methodological inadequacies.) In addition, although there is little systematic research to support such claims, LGAT brochures promise results such as "gains in self-esteem, openness and vitality, greater participation and enjoyment in the daily activities of life, more effective leadership, greater willingness to be responsible, and a renewed sense of direction and purpose" (Lifespring, 1985, p. 3). Another LGAT claims that it provides "a breakthrough in personal effectiveness, a breakthrough in the practice of excellence, a breakthrough in the art and science of achievement" (Werner Erhard & Associates, 1988, p. 1).

The claims of LGAT proponents notwithstanding, LGAT opponents are concerned about hazardous outcomes. Fenwick (1976) feared that the confrontational techniques used in LGATs would "undermine psychological defenses and strip away resistance...increase anxiety...(and) encourage regression to developmentally primitive modes of functioning" (p. 171). Others are concerned that participation may lead to undermined ego functions, reasoning disturbances, regressions, and infantilizing (Haaken & Adams, 1983). Finally, some caution that these effects could lead to broader negative societal consequences (cf. Cinnamon & Farson, 1979; Conway & Siegelman, 1978). Again, however, there is presently little rigorous scientific evidence to support such fears.

Past LGAT Outcome Research

Past LGAT outcome studies have involved several types of research: (1) case studies of psychological outcome, (2) descriptive outcome surveys, and (3) pre- and post-treatment, self-report studies.[3] Although much of this work addresses issues related to the controversy surrounding LGATs, most is plagued with methodological inadequacies which preclude definitive conclusions.

Case Studies of Psychological Outcome

A number of case study reports have described alleged LGAT-induced casualties, while others have described alleged LGAT-induced benefits. Concerning casualties, there is little agreement among mental health professionals about how to define a casualty or about how to measure psychological disturbances which could result from LGAT participation, and different studies have approached these issues in different ways (cf. Cartwright & Vogel, 1960; Garfield & Bergin, 1971; Ling, Zausmer, & Hope, 1952). Lieberman et al. (1973) defined the term "casualty" as referring to people (1) who function in day-to-day life in a significantly less effective manner after the LGAT than prior to it, (2) who are affected on a long-term basis by their decreased functioning, and (3) who can associate this inferior functioning directly to the LGAT experience. Although these conditions seem essential to attribute psychological harm to LGAT participation unambiguously, they have rarely been met in extant research.

Some case studies are of people who were referred to mental health units following LGAT participation. Others are of clinicians' observations of their patients who had participated in LGATs. In this vein, Glass, Kirsch, and Parris (1977) and Kirsch and Glass (1977) described a total of seven cases of psychiatric disturbances that were purported to have developed soon after participation in the *est* training.

Other case studies have been more equivocal. For example, Simon (1978) reported the outcome of 49 patients who were advised by the author to participate in the *est* training during the course of therapy. He concluded that only one client with a previous history of mental illness showed transient psychotic symptoms after the LGAT experience. Of the other patients, 30 appeared clinically improved, and the remaining 18 appeared to be unchanged by the experience. Hamsher (*est*, 1977) interviewed mental health professionals who were graduates of LGATs, most of whom treated clients who had also participated in LGATs. He reported that overall, most of the professionals believed the LGAT experience was beneficial to many of their clients, with the exception of those clients with severe mental disorders (e.g., compensated psychotics).

More recently, Lieberman (1987) employed a more structured research design in his study of LGAT outcomes. The author selected 30 participants from the Lifespring basic training who comprised a "high risk" group in that they seemed more likely than others to be harmed by LGAT participation. The method for identifying this group of individuals included administering a series of psychological instruments prior to the training, observing participants during the training

---

[3]The term "treatment" as used here and throughout this volume refers to an experimental condition, and does not imply that LGAT is regarded by the authors as a form of therapeutic treatment.

(looking for erratic behavior, stress responses, etc.), and having participants nominate anyone at the end of the training "who they believed had been overly distressed, hurt, harmed, or disturbed" (p. 462). The high risk individuals who could be contacted and who agreed to the interview were evaluated three or four weeks after the LGAT experience and again after three years. Clinical interviews and the Diagnostic Interview Schedule were used to evaluate these individuals subjectively and objectively. Although seven out of the 11 participants completing both interviews met the criteria for lifetime pathology, the report concluded that there was no evidence that this was related to LGAT participation, because the participants' post-LGAT conditions appeared to be similar to what they had been prior to participation.

Although case studies may be useful for identifying the types of beneficial and harmful outcomes that could possibly be associated with LGATs, the methodology is quite limited (Campbell & Stanley, 1966). To begin with, case studies generally involve a self-selected population (e.g., those who present to a therapist with psychological distress shortly after LGAT participation, or clients referred to LGAT by their psychotherapist), which may not be representative of LGAT participants as a whole. Thus, case studies cannot provide a good indication of the proportion of participants who may be harmed or who may benefit. In addition, the evaluations are usually based on clinical impressions rather than objective measurements. Thus, they reflect the views of individual professionals, who may be influenced by their personal opinions of LGATs. Also, because no objective comparison is generally made between the psychological states of participants before and after the LGAT, the purported negative consequences or benefits often cannot be attributed directly to LGAT participation.

Descriptive Outcome Surveys

A number of descriptive surveys of LGATs have attempted to assess outcomes following LGAT participation. These studies typically involve individuals completing evaluations of LGAT outcome after its completion. In a study by Ornstein, Swencionis, Deikman, and Morris (1975), about 1200 *est* participants were asked to evaluate areas relating to their current physical and mental health as compared to the year prior to LGAT participation. Respondents reported improved general health, less sleep difficulties, a decrease in the use of addictive substances (e.g., drugs, alcohol, and cigarettes), fewer headaches and migraines, and less frequent periods of irritation, anxiety, and depression. In addition, Ross asked 382 participants in the Lifespring basic training and 289 individuals in the advanced Lifespring training to evaluate certain aspects of the program (i.e., interest, instructor behavior, etc.). According to the report, the vast majority of the respondents judged the program very positively (Lifespring, 1986).

At best, descriptive outcome surveys can be informative regarding participant satisfaction with various LGAT programs. They may even document the participants' tendency to view themselves as having profited, sometimes dramatically, from the experience. However, it is not valid to assume that the purported benefits, such as those described by Ornstein et al. (1975) and Lifespring (1986), occurred as reported. Since such studies include only post-measures, there is no baseline against which to compare the reported changes and no independent evidence that they do, in fact, represent change. Even if pre-post changes were observed, without a control group of individuals who did not participate in the LGAT, it would be impossible to determine unambiguously whether the effects occurred as a result of LGAT participation. Research designs involving pre- and post-measures, as well as an appropriate control group, are necessary to eliminate these interpretive difficulties (Campbell & Stanley, 1966).

Descriptive outcome surveys are also characterized by serious "demand characteristics" and "response set" problems (cf. Fowler, 1984; Sudman & Bradburn, 1974). In situations where the respondent knows or suspects that the research is connected with the organization sponsoring the LGAT, he or she may feel compelled to respond in a way that does not reflect his or her true attitude but one that is perceived as "socially desirable". This can seriously undermine the conclusions that can be drawn from such research (Rosenberg, 1969; Tedeschi, Schlenker, & Bonoma, 1971). In fact, McCardel and Murray (1974) suggested that "response set" may sometimes be an even more powerful determinant of research results than the active ingredients of a personal growth intervention.

A second, related problem can arise in descriptive assessments made by participants following LGAT participation. It has been found that in order to justify their behavior, people who exert a large effort to join an activity may represent themselves as more enthusiastic about the activity than those who exert less effort (e.g., Aronson & Mills, 1959). Since LGATs are often expensive, require a considerable amount of time, and may even subject the individual to ridicule from his or her peers, they can be considered a "high effort" activity. As a result, there may be a tendency for respondents to overemphasize the effectiveness of the LGAT experience in order to justify the effort. This may yield effects that appear to be due to the LGAT but which are not. If the study involves the respondent comparing his or her condition before and after the LGAT experience, such effects may be intensified, because retrospective self-reports tend to indicate change from the past to the present, even when none, in fact, has occurred. Studies suggest that individuals comparing the past to the present tend to exaggerate past misfortune so that current conditions appear to be improved (Frank, 1961; Richardson, Stewart, & Simmonds, 1978; Ross & Conway, 1984). Some of the aforementioned criticisms apply to the studies discussed in the next section as well.

Pre-Post Treatment Self-Report Studies

A third set of studies assessing the psychological outcome of LGAT participation have involved the use of pre- and post-treatment self-reports. Although these studies often utilize well-validated psychological instruments, are more sophisticated methodologically than case studies or descriptive outcome studies, and on occasion have even included control groups, they still have serious methodological limitations.

The earliest pre-post study of LGAT participation was conducted by Behaviordyne (Tondow, Teague, Finney, & LeMaistre, 1973) and involved administering the California Psychological Inventory (CPI) to *est* participants pre-training, immediately post-training, and three months post-training. This study included a no-treatment control group of individuals matched on age, sex, and socio-economic status. Results suggested that LGAT participants exhibited improved self-image and lower anxiety, guilt, and dependency and that the control group evidenced no significant changes. However, because the pre- and post-measures for the control group were never directly compared to those of the experimental group, it is difficult to determine the validity of these conclusions (see Finkelstein et al., 1982). When an 18-month follow-up was conducted on some of the Tondow et al. (1973) subjects, it yielded little reliable information on the long-term effects of *est* participation (Lewis, 1976).

A study by Weiss (1977) examined *est* graduates pre- and post-training in relation to members of a "waiting list" control group which had not yet participated in the training. The results indicated positive effects of *est* participation for some of the dependent measures assessed (i.e., decreased self-concept incongruency for females and decreased average level of distress). However, these effects were only short-term. In addition, the waiting list control group used was inadequate because it was not randomly assigned and included only a small number of individuals who were evaluated at a different location and at a different time from the treatment group. Although Hazen (1980) retested Weiss' subjects at 18-month and 3-year intervals, methodological inadequacies precluded any conclusion about long-term effects.

A study by Hartke (1980) assessed whether the *est* training led to changes in ego development. From a larger group of *est* participants, 86 agreed to participate in the research and completed the pre-test. Subjects were tested two weeks prior to the training, two weeks after the training, and again three months post-training. Results suggested significant increases in ego-development following LGAT participation. However, since no control group was used in this study, the validity of the results is difficult to interpret.

Although the above studies were methodologically superior to previous research, they still contained major design flaws. In addition to the problem of inadequate control groups, subjects in all the studies were aware that the research was designed to document changes due to LGAT participation. As a result, the problems with experimental demand and response set noted earlier may have influenced the findings.

Another problem with many pre-post studies of LGAT outcome and other types of LGAT outcome studies as well, is that they have often focused on only one dimension (e.g., changes in personality) in assessing possible LGAT effects. A multidimensional approach would be more desirable because it would allow the measurement of the broad range of outcomes that may be associated with LGAT participation. Relying on personality measures as the sole indicator of outcome is especially problematic because there is often similarity between the issues stressed in the LGAT (e.g., personal responsibility) and the content of the personality measure in question (e.g., locus of control). Under such conditions, changes reflected in a personality inventory could be the result of learning a new set of convictions, rather than the result of actual personality change.

Summary of Past Research

Overall, a review of LGAT outcome research reveals several inherent problems. First, most studies lack an adequate control group. Second, few designs employ pre- and post-measures where appropriate. Third, most research has paid inadequate attention to response set bias. Each of these methodological weaknesses makes it difficult to generate clear causal inferences from the studies which have been conducted to date. Thus, it is impossible to assess whether or not LGAT participation is responsible for *any* reported effects. Moreover, prior research has failed to include outcome assessments of multiple dimensions.

Design Considerations in LGAT Research

Although some of the aforementioned methodological inadequacies are relatively simple to alleviate, others are more complex. Unfortunately, possible solutions sometimes involve "exchanging" one problem for another (Cook & Campbell, 1979). For example, controlled studies that include pre- and post-test measurements may allow one to assess whether change actually resulted from an LGAT experience, but can cause an interaction of testing by treatment. This is the possibility that the pre-testing "sensitizes" the subject to the impending treatment and affects its effectiveness, perhaps by making the participant more aware of his or her initial psychological state. Thus, although the use of pre-post measures may give the researcher a sounder basis on which to document the existence of an LGAT treatment effect, it also becomes plausible that the pre-measure helped to cause it. A careful consideration of such issues is essential in order to comprehend fully the difficult and complex choices faced by investigators of LGATs in their attempts to design more effective LGAT outcome studies.

In the following section, some of the major methodological issues relevant to designing LGAT outcome research and various ways of addressing them are discussed systematically. First, we consider the need to include an adequate control group in LGAT outcome research. We then address the issue of utilizing pre-post measures when necessary. Third, we consider the advantage of assessing multiple LGAT outcome indicators. Finally, we address the need to minimize response set bias in LGAT outcome research.

Providing an Adequate Control Group

Without an adequate control group, one cannot rule out alternative explanations for any effects observed in LGAT outcome research. For example, LGAT outcomes may actually be due to historical events that influenced the general public (as well as LGAT participants), or simply due to maturational processes experienced by everyone, not just LGAT participants. Effects may also be a result of measurement artifacts such as "regression to the mean", as when subjects elect treatment when especially unhappy, so that improvement over time is inevitable (cf. Campbell & Stanley, 1966; Cook & Campbell, 1979). Finally, effects may be due to what is termed "spontaneous recovery" in psychotherapy research, or the tendency to get better over time without therapeutic intervention (Bergin, 1971).

Unless a group participating in a LGAT differs from an appropriate "no treatment" control group following treatment, the above possibilities, as well as others, cannot be ruled out. Ideally, then, LGAT outcome should be studied with a design involving the random assignment of subjects to a LGAT treatment condition and to a "no treatment" control group. This, along with other experimental controls, allows unambiguous causal inferences about LGAT effects. Since the subjects in the two groups may be assumed to be equivalent (and other factors not related to the intervention that affect people's outcomes, such as history or maturation, may be assumed to be equivalent as well), the only difference between them is attendance at LGAT sessions. This increases the likelihood that it is the treatment and not another factor that has caused any differential outcome between conditions (Campbell & Stanley, 1966; Cook & Campbell, 1979).

Unfortunately, random assignment to treatment and control groups is fraught with complications for the evaluation of LGAT outcomes. It would be difficult to assign randomly individuals who want to become involved in LGAT either to participate in a LGAT group or to be in a traditional "no treatment" control group. These people are highly motivated to take the LGAT, have sought it out, and are often willing to pay a substantial amount of money to participate. Most likely, they would be quite unwilling to agree not to participate, and even if they did, such a group might be characterized by resentment, making them an inappropriate control (Cook & Campbell, 1979). In addition, it would be difficult to convince LGAT organizations, which are run for profit, to agree to deny participation to people interested in the LGAT.

One way to guarantee random assignment to a LGAT and to a "no treatment" control condition would be to use volunteer subjects or subjects solicited from the general population, instead of those with an expressed interest in LGAT. Since the former have no commitment to attending LGAT, one could more easily assign them randomly to a LGAT treatment or a "no treatment" control group. However, the external validity of these data would be limited. This is because such subjects are probably unlike the population that normally participates in LGATs. Volunteer subjects or individuals obtained from the general population might differ from typical LGAT participants on personality and socio-demographic variables, in their motivation for or readiness to accept treatment, or on other dimensions. If no change were observed, it could be because they had no need to change, were less involved, had lower expectations for results, etc. If the data indicated the treatment caused no harm, it could be claimed that the subjects were not representative of LGAT clients, who might be more vulnerable. Although using such subjects would yield the potential for random assignment and experimental control, ecological and external validity would be sacrificed. Since researchers are interested in the effect of LGATs on the population that normally enrolls in them, rather than on the general population, such a compromise is unwarranted.

The use of a "waiting list" control group. An alternative method for providing random assignment to treatment and to no treatment conditions involves using a "waiting list" control group. This method is sometimes used in therapy research and permits the assessment of possible LGAT effects on the population that normally involves itself in LGAT. In this design, LGAT applicants are randomly assigned to the first available LGAT or to a later one. While the former group receives treatment, the waiting list group serves as a no treatment control and is measured at the same intervals as the treatment group. Subjects in the two groups can be assumed to be comparable (cf. Subotnik, 1972).

By comparing the responses of subjects in the experimental and in the waiting list control group, the effects of treatment can be assessed. Such comparisons also distinguish the portion of an effect attributable to the treatment from that resulting from expectancies for improvement (Frank, 1961; Goldstein, 1960; Murray & Jacobson, 1971). In addition, the design helps distinguish changes due to treatment from those that could occur without treatment, such as spontaneous recovery (Bergin, 1971) or "regression to the mean" (Campbell & Stanley, 1966). In both cases, comparison between the LGAT and waiting list groups would indicate each to have improved. Without such a comparison, it might have been concluded that LGAT participation was responsible for the observed effects.

Unfortunately, using a waiting list control group is complicated by practical and ethical issues. Temporarily denying subjects participation in a treatment they may feel they need could have detrimental effects on them (cf. Cook & Campbell, 1979; Kidder & Judd, 1986). The delay might even create anger or resentment toward the LGAT and could impact on the person's eventual response to it (cf. Aubrey, 1987; Campbell & Stanley, 1966; Garfield, 1987). Each of these processes could affect the adequacy of the waiting list control by making it non-equivalent to the LGAT treatment group. Non-equivalence could occur in other ways as well. Waiting list subjects may not remain untreated but may seek alternative treatment rather than wait to participate in the LGAT (Frank, 1961; Powers & Witmer, 1951). Subjects who register for a program and encounter a delay may also drop out—yielding a non-equivalent control group selectively diminished by attrition.

Other considerations may also complicate the picture. Unlike interventions in institutional settings where researchers have control over client allocation to experimental conditions, LGATs are commercial organizations and are more sensitive to client reactions.[4] Postponing LGAT applicants for a waiting list control group could result in a possible loss of income, client good will, or both. Also, because family members or friends sometimes register for the LGAT together, it is possible for the waiting list subjects to question why they have been referred to a later training, while others have not. This could affect the researchers' and/or the LGAT's credibility. A final limitation on the waiting list control is that it can be employed only in short-term experiments. Since subjects eventually receive the treatment, they cannot serve as a control group in the evaluation of long-term LGAT effects.

A placebo or pseudo-therapy control group. Finkelstein et al. (1982) argue that, in addition to a no treatment control group, in order to research LGAT outcome effectively, there should be another control group that undergoes a "pseudo-treatment". Assignment to this condition should also be based on random assign-ment. The "placebo" group should be "exposed to an intense, focused experi-ence capable of creating powerful response sets" (Finkelstein et al., 1982, p. 526) and would serve two purposes: to control for subjects reporting improvement simply because they believe it is socially desirable to do so (i.e., response sets), and to distinguish between effects resulting from aspects specific to the LGAT and effects resulting from non-specific aspects (e.g., group enthusiasm, expectations for improvement, non-judgmental relationships formed among group members, etc.) (cf. McCardel & Murray, 1974).

---

[4]To date, the only application of a truly randomized waiting list control group in LGAT outcome research was among inmates in a prison (Hosford, Moss, Cavior, & Kernish, 1980), where control over subjects is maximal.

Controlling for response sets is very relevant to the present, initial phase of LGAT outcome research, in which researchers are attempting to ascertain whether or not LGATs produce effects. A placebo control would serve to identify the response set problem because, if it were operating, it would occur in both the control and experimental groups. However, using a placebo group presents practical and ethical problems even more serious than those resulting from the use of a waiting list control. For a discussion of some of the problems associated with placebo control groups, see Cook and Campbell (1979). We will discuss some of the most relevant issues below.

First, for the researcher, creating an "intense and focused experience" and presenting it as an LGAT could be difficult and costly and could involve liability issues. In addition, an LGAT organization would justifiably be hesitant to present the placebo control treatment as its own. Second, since most candidates are at least somewhat familiar with the particular LGAT for which they are registering, it would be difficult to assign LGAT registrants to the placebo control group without their recognizing that the treatment is false. This would considerably diminish the placebo value of such a group. Fortunately, it is possible to control for response set bias without using a placebo control. Disassociating the LGAT evaluation from the LGAT treatment can eliminate the primary cause of response set bias and avoid the above complications. (For specifics on how this may be accomplished, see Chapter 2.)

As noted above, the second possible function of a placebo control group is that it enables the researcher to distinguish between a treatment's specific and non-specific effects. Although this issue is also very relevant to LGAT research, at present such a use of a placebo would be premature. If LGATs do show reliable treatment effects in the initial phase of LGAT outcome research, it would then become useful to isolate the specific "active ingredients" of LGATs. However, the proper use of this technique would first require a considerable amount of conceptual work to attempt to understand how LGATs achieve their effects. Since there are many potential, significant aspects of LGAT treatment (e.g., the content, the leadership style, the opportunity for self-disclosure), it is likely that it would be necessary to use multiple control groups in which the various elements were varied systematically.

The use of a non-equivalent control group design. To this point, all of the types of control groups which we have discussed have involved random assignment. Although approaches involving random assignment to LGAT treatment or to appropriate control conditions offer the greatest opportunity to make unambiguous causal inferences about LGAT outcome, we have indicated that there are significant practical difficulties in their application (e.g., randomly assigning individuals interested in attending a LGAT either to the LGAT, or to a no treatment control group, is problematic). An alternative to assigning subjects randomly to treatment and control groups is the use of a non-equivalent control group design (see Cook

& Campbell, 1979; Judd & Kenny, 1981). In this design, the experimental and control groups are not randomly determined and, therefore, are not equivalent. Even though the two groups are non-equivalent, the control group may be used to rule out certain alternative explanations for the results. Rather than being a "true" experimental design, such a design is referred to as "quasi-experimental" (Campbell & Stanley, 1966).

Given the constraint of non-random assignment, the quasi-experimental research designs and appropriate statistical analyses enable researchers to assess treatment effects as unambiguously as possible. Careful use of such techniques allows researchers to attempt a relatively unbiased estimate of a treatment's effect in a field setting characterized by "real life" constraints, though with a lower degree of certainty than in "true" experimental research. This is done by considering the various threats to internal validity occasioned by non-random assignment and attempting to compensate for them both in the generation of the control group(s) and in the statistical analysis of the data. Although the use of quasi-experimentation in LGAT outcome research involves lower internal validity than a true experiment, a true experiment might actually be characterized by lower external and ecological validity. This is because random assignment to treatment and control groups would require the researcher to alter the process by which people enroll in and participate in LGATs, or to use different subject populations than those characteristic of LGATs.

Using Pre-Post Measures When Necessary

As noted earlier, in addition to problems with control groups or the absence of any control group at all, other methodological inadequacies have characterized past LGAT outcome research. For example, few LGAT outcome studies have included pre- and post-measures when these would have been appropriate. Although such measures are not critical in true experiments, since randomization eliminates initial differences between treatment and control groups, they are necessary in other contexts. For example, some LGAT outcome studies have involved post-only designs without any control group. Although this is an extremely weak design, it could have been strengthened slightly by including pre-post measurements. Other studies have utilized post-only designs in conjunction with non-equivalent control groups. When using any quasi-experimental design, there will be a degree of non-equivalence between groups. A pre-test provides a baseline to differentiate between initial differences between the groups and those caused by the treatment of the experimental group (Cook & Campbell, 1979; Rossi, Freeman, & Wright, 1979). Since the pre-test may "sensitize" the subject and affect his or her response to the LGAT (Solomon, 1949), the researcher can randomly assign some experimental subjects to receive only the post-test, to assess the effect of pre-testing on treatment. Any difference between the post-test only and the pre-post test group would indicate that pre-testing affected treatment.

Using Multiple Outcome Indicators

A third problem in past LGAT outcome research is that only a limited range of potential outcomes have been assessed. Past studies have generally focused on *one* of the following outcome domains: (1) personality changes, particularly in self-concept (Hartke, 1980; Hazan, 1980; Tondow et al., 1973; Weiss, 1977), (2) potential psychological harm (Lieberman, 1987), and (3) effects on physical well-being (Ornstein et al., 1975). Given the nature of potential LGAT outcomes, a more global assessment would be preferred. Employing a variety of psychological instruments representing different constructs could effectively measure many potential outcomes and minimize the likelihood of the researcher overlooking possible effects. It also permits the specification of models of LGAT outcome.

Minimizing Response Set Bias

A final problem identified in past research involves "response sets," which can occur when subjects perceive the purpose of LGAT outcome research or become aware of a connection between the research and an LGAT organization. One frequently used method of assessing the extent of the response set problem involves including a measure of "social desirability" (i.e., of subjects' tendency to report their behavior so it will appear favorably to others), along with other measurement instruments (see Crowne & Marlowe, 1960). Such a measure could also be used as a covariate, or as a factor in subsequent analyses. Another approach is to attempt to lessen the likelihood of response set bias through elements of the experimental design. As noted earlier, response sets can be diminished considerably if LGAT outcome studies are conducted so that they are not associated with the LGAT experience or with the LGAT organization. Measuring LGAT effects using a context disassociated from the LGAT has not been attempted in past research.

Another aspect of the response set problem is related to the nature of the instruments employed rather than the context of the research. Measures that focus directly on issues emphasized in the LGAT program, that ask for opinions about values central to the program, or that use a similar terminology are most problematic. For such measures, there is danger of a "parroting effect", i.e., that the subject will merely repeat what he or she was taught in the LGAT experience. Unfortunately, the outcome variables of major interest in the better-controlled LGAT outcome studies to date (e.g., personality changes involving increased self-esteem) are among those most in danger of such response set problems. As the authors themselves sometimes suggest, there is an undeniable similarity between the issues discussed in LGAT (e.g., an emphasis on the importance of high self-esteem, the dangers of stereotypic thinking), and the contents of the instruments measuring such constructs (Hartke, 1980). Although this should not preclude using these variables in research, it suggests using multiple measures and not relying on them as sole indicators of LGAT-induced change.

The Current Research

Up to this point, no LGAT outcome studies have dealt effectively with the complex methodological issues discussed above. Although it would be unreasonable to expect a single study to deal with all these problems simultaneously, it is important to attempt LGAT outcome research that is methodologically stronger than extant work. In addition to helping to resolve the LGAT controversies mentioned earlier, Finkelstein et al. (1982) mention several important, additional reasons for studying LGATs more carefully: (a) the great numbers of participants in LGATs indicate that many people's needs are being met "neither by society nor by the traditional psychotherapy disciplines" (p. 517), (b) many therapists will treat clients who have been through such training or who will become involved in it during their therapy, and (c) such research may suggest useful techniques that could be incorporated into more traditional therapies or that may help to develop certain aspects of personality theory.

Additionally, the study of LGATs may offer a considerable contribution to social and community psychology. LGAT studies address some classic concerns of these fields, such as social influence (cf. Cialdini, 1984) and large group effects (Paulus, 1980; Zander, 1985). Also, because LGATs may be attractive to people seeking personal change, a study of LGATs could lead to the development of a social psychological perspective on change. Personal change has been discussed by some writers, but usually from a broad cultural and societal perspective (e.g., Beit-Hallahmi, 1987; Zilbergeld, 1983), rather than a social psychological one. A related issue which has recently received much attention is the formation and functioning of social support systems (e.g., Gottlieb, 1988), and studying LGATs might reveal functions that traditional social support systems are failing to satisfy.

With the dual goals of providing a methodologically stronger LGAT outcome evaluation than past research and making a contribution to social, clinical and community psychology, a study was designed to assess the effect of the Forum. As the successor to the *est* training, the Forum is considered a prototype of many LGATs of the late 1980's and has attracted a significant number of participants since being introduced in 1985 (Werner Erhard & Associates, 1989).[5] This is the first outcome study to focus on the Forum, and it is methodologically superior to past LGAT outcome research. It utilizes a pre-post design; includes a control group that allows the effects of Forum participation to be distinguished from the effects of history, maturation, etc.; and minimizes response set bias by utilizing a research context disassociated from the LGAT. In addition, a multidimensional approach to outcome assessment has been adopted.

---

[5]While the Forum is considered by some to be a prototype of other LGATs, the degree of uniqueness or similarity of the Forum to the *est* training or to any other large group intervention is beyond the scope of this volume.

Chapter II
Study Methods

Overview of the Methods Employed

The present study of Forum outcome was conducted within a large scale investigation of the Quality of Life in North America. A quasi-experimental, non-equivalent control group design was used to assess the short- and long-term effects of participation in the Forum. The *experimental subjects* consisted of men and women who attended Forum seminars during 1985, in a large city in the northeastern United States. About two-thirds were assigned to Group 1 and were asked to complete and return questionnaires both prior to the Forum and after Forum participation. The remaining experimental subjects constituted Group 2, and were asked to complete an identical questionnaire only *after* Forum participation. This group was included to test for the interaction of treatment and testing. Both groups were administered a follow-up questionnaire approximately a year and one-half after Forum participation to assess its long-term effects.

When first contacted, each subject in Groups 1 and 2 was asked to nominate another person whom the subject knew and believed was "similar to him- or herself." These individuals constituted the *nominee control group* (Group 3) and were asked by the researchers to participate in the study. Those that accepted were sent the identical questionnaires at similar time intervals as subjects in Group 1. Nominees who had already participated in the Forum or the *est* training were eliminated from the control group. The design is presented schematically in Table 2.1.

The questionnaires used for all the experimental and control subjects included a battery of standardized, psychometrically sound instruments. The study for which subjects completed the questionnaires was entitled "The Quality of Life in North America." In addition to assessing Forum outcome, the data were used for a wider series of investigations of social well-being (see, e.g., Klar, Mendola, Fisher, Silver, Chinsky, & Goff, 1990). No specific reference was made to the Forum in the description of the study or in its contents. Subjects completed an informed consent document before participating in the research.

Research Design

The research was designed to measure subjects' responses to Forum participation at three intervals. To obtain a baseline for all the variables under study, the first

Table 2.1. Experimental Design

	Pre-test		Post-test	Follow-up
Group 1 (Forum Participants)	0_1	x	0_2	0_3
Group 2 (Forum Participants)		x	0_4	0_5
– –
Group 3 (Nominees)	0_6		0_7	0_8

Note: In the above diagram, the subscripts indicate measurements and the x's denote the Forum intervention. The dashed line separating the treated and the comparison groups indicates that the groups were not formed on the basis of random assignment to conditions.

measures were administered four to six weeks prior to participation in the Forum. The second measurement was administered four to six weeks after completing the Forum, in order to assess the short-term effects of participation. A third measurement occurred approximately a year and one-half after Forum participation, to evaluate its long-term effects as well as the stability of any short-term effects that may have been observed.

Elements of both true and quasi-experimentation were initially built into the design of the study. Specifically, in addition to Forum participants and a non-equivalent control group (i.e., the nominee control group, which was chosen to be as similar as possible to the experimental group), there was to be a randomized, waiting list control group. However, it soon became evident that, in the present research context, the use of a waiting list control was not viable.[1] Because of this, only the non-equivalent, nominee control group was retained in the final design. Since Forum subjects and individuals in the non-equivalent control group were not randomly assigned to treatment and to control conditions, the research involved a quasi-experimental, non-equivalent control group design (Cook & Campbell, 1979).

The non-equivalent control group design. Non-equivalent control group (NECG) designs have been widely utilized in field research. According to Judd and Kenny (1981), this "archetypal quasi-experimental design is often the most internally valid design that many researchers can implement in applied settings" (p. 103). One of the traditional methods used in the non-equivalent control group design for obtaining a comparable, though nonequivalent, control group is the *matching technique* (Greenwood, 1945; Selltiz, Jahoda, Deutsch, & Cook, 1959). Using this method, the researcher selects control subjects based on their similarity to experimental subjects on certain variables believed to be relevant to the study (e.g., gender, age, IQ).

There are several difficulties associated with this method. When the experimental group is unique in some way, it is difficult to determine what variables need to be similar to produce a comparable control group (Campbell & Boruch, 1975; Campbell & Erlebacher, 1970). For example, in choosing a comparison group for a LGAT outcome study, the researchers could not be certain *a priori* on which variables to match because it is unclear which factors lead individuals to select themselves into LGATs (but see Klar et al., 1990). In addition, the matching technique can be expensive and time-consuming because it requires contacting large numbers of potential subjects, screening them to determine who is appropriate for the control group, and recontacting those who are eligible (Rossi et al.,

---

[1]The "waiting list" design was created such that one third of the prospective Forum participants would be asked to register for a later, rather than the next available, Forum date. (No mention of the next available date was made to them.) However, it readily became clear that this was not an effective method for randomly assigning subjects to different conditions. Many subjects were aware of the dates the Forum was to take place and insisted on participating in the next available one, rather than in a later session. To avoid credibility problems and the loss of potential participants, Forum registrars were instructed not to argue or to try to persuade such applicants to enroll in the later Forum. Enrollment of subjects in the waiting list control group was terminated as soon as it was clear that this would not be a viable group. Although 11 subjects (out of 19 that initially agreed to participate in this condition before it was discontinued) completed both pre- and post-measures, they were dropped from the study and their data were not used, since the number of subjects was too small to serve as a reliable comparison group.

1979). With a demographically heterogeneous experimental group, it is especially difficult to generate a comparable control group because the researcher has to create a group of control subjects with diverse backgrounds. Finally, even though the treatment and control groups may match on the variables selected, the groups may not be comparable on other relevant variables (Rossi et al., 1979). It is unlikely that a group chosen by the researcher based on a single, specific variable or a small set of variables would prove to be comparable in an overall sense.

A less problematic method for selecting a non-equivalent control group is the *peer nomination technique.* This is a recently developed quasi-experimental technique for creating a comparable (although non-randomly assigned) control group, which emanated from the matching technique. This method is unique because the experimental subjects, rather than the researcher, select the control subjects based on instructions given by the researcher (e.g., to select others they know who are similar to themselves and of the same gender, age, and socio-economic status). Previous research (Sharp, 1985) proved the efficiency and lower expense of this method in generating a demographically comparable control group. The peer nomination technique is especially efficacious when generating a control group that is comparable to an experimental group that is unique and/or heterogeneous. In addition to producing a demographically matched control group, this technique can yield one which is comparable on other dimensions. If the experimental subject is asked to nominate a person who he or she considers "similar to him- or herself," it is likely that the resultant control subject will be comparable on demographic, personality and other dimensions.

Although peer nomination does not guarantee that the subjects nominated will be similar to the experimental subjects on the dimensions relevant to LGAT outcome research, it is likely to offer a better approximation than the "matching technique"—especially since there is an inadequate knowledge base about the personality, lifestyle, and attitudinal factors associated with LGAT participation on which control subjects could be pre-selected. Peer nomination methods have been used successfully in many areas of psychological and educational research (though not typically for the present purposes, i.e., to create a comparable control group), and subjects have demonstrated considerable ability to nominate peers according to specific personality characteristics (cf. Lazarus & Weinstock, 1984; Lefkowitz & Tesiny, 1985; Paterson, Dickson, & Layne, 1984; Shoemaker, Erickson, & Finch, 1986), and in order to fulfill specific roles (e.g., Tziner & Dolan, 1982).

Although the peer nomination method can be used to obtain a degree of comparability, it should be complemented with appropriate statistical methods, as with any non-equivalent control group technique. To the extent that the experimental and peer-nominated control groups are non-comparable, multivariate statistical methods (e.g., structural equation modeling) can estimate and control for such differences and increase the internal validity of the analysis.

Experimental Procedures

Contacting Forum participants. The initial contact between the researchers and potential Forum participants in the study occurred under the auspices of the Forum organization. Between August and December 1985, a letter was included in the registration packets of all Forum registrants in a large northeastern city informing them about a study on the Quality of Life in North America being performed by researchers from the University of Connecticut and the University of Waterloo, Canada. It was stated that, among the segments of the population to be included in the study, individuals participating in large group awareness trainings would be represented. The purpose of the study was explained to prospective subjects as follows:

> The research has been developed to contribute to an understanding of some factors affecting the quality of people's lives. We will be asking how people have been feeling lately, how they spend their free time, and the impact of various life experiences.

The context of the overall study was thus almost entirely dissociated from the context of LGAT evaluation. As a result, the potential for response bias was minimized.

Subjects were promised anonymity and confidentiality and it was stressed that participation in the study was strictly voluntary. Forum participants who preferred not to be contacted for the research were asked to mail an enclosed, stamped, self-addressed postcard to the Forum organization, requesting that their name not be released to the research team. Researchers phoned those individuals who made themselves available for contact no later than six weeks prior to the Forum for which they had registered, and asked whether or not they would be willing to participate in the study by completing questionnaires on two separate occasions (or on only one occasion in the case of Group 2). (At this point, the one and one-half year follow-up study was not mentioned to subjects.) Prospective subjects were informed that each questionnaire would take approximately 45-60 minutes to complete and that they would receive $15 for their overall participation. Those Forum registrants available for contact were asked to complete the questionnaire by dates that were four weeks pre-Forum (for Group 1) and four weeks post-Forum (for Groups 1 and 2). To ensure a sufficient number of experimental subjects, participants for the study were recruited from several succeeding Forums, and the identical procedures were used for each successive group.

To be eligible for inclusion in the research, experimental subjects had to have registered for the Forum at least six weeks prior to the one under study, to have been contacted by telephone by our research team more than four weeks prior to the Forum and invited to participate, to have paid the Forum registration fee, to have never previously attended the Forum or *est*, and to have actually attended the Forum in its entirety (across two weekend sessions).

Of the 685 prospective participants who received letters describing the study, 224 returned postcards indicating they did not wish to be contacted, or were unwilling to participate when called. Another 151 prospective participants could not be reached by phone within the time interval in which the calls were made, despite at least two, and often several, attempts.

Three hundred-ten prospective participants agreed by phone to complete questionnaire packets and received the first questionnaire.[2] Of these, 107 ultimately did not meet our requirements for eligibility, and 19 others had been assigned to the waiting-list control group, which as noted earlier, was discontinued.[3] Forty-nine eligible subjects did not return one or more of the pre- or post-test packets within the designated time frames, despite our mailing reminder letters at five and 10-day intervals, and following up with a phone call 10 days post-mailing. Overall, 83 individuals in Group 1 completed and returned pre- and post-test measures and 52 in Group 2 completed post-test measures.

Contacting the nominees. In the initial telephone contact, each prospective Forum participant who agreed to take part in the "Quality of Life Study" was asked to nominate an other for participation in the research who was of the same gender, of approximately the same age, from the same community, and whom the participant considered to be "like him- or herself". The participant was asked not to nominate his or her best friend or anyone who lived in the participant's household. The 244 individuals who were nominated in this way were contacted by mail and offered the same financial compensation ($15) for completing the pre- and post-test measures. Of these, 59 could not be reached during the designed time frame despite at least two, and often several attempts, and 32 refused to participate. One hundred fifty-three nominees were mailed questionnaires. Of this group, 22 were excluded because of prior LGAT experience. Seventy-three of the remaining potential respondents returned pre- and post-test packets within the period of

---

[2]Comparisons were conducted between those Forum participants who agreed to participate and all other Forum participants in the same geographic area during the same time period to look for indications of selective participation. The following variables were compared: (1) number of hours in Forum-related activities after the completion of the Forum (a measure of involvement in the Forum), (2) family status (i.e., being married, single, divorced or separated at the beginning of the Forum), (3) education level, and (4) income level. These comparisons yielded no significant differences between the two groups. Thus, based on this data there is no reason to assume that Forum participants who agreed to participate in our research were significantly different from Forum participants overall.

[3]Of the subjects who were ineligible for inclusion, 72 dropped out of the Forum, 21 transferred to a later Forum, and 14 had previously participated in the Forum or *est*.

eligibility.[4] The timing of nominee assessments was yoked to the pre- and post-tests of Forum subjects.

The follow-up study. For the year and one-half follow-up study, subjects who indicated at the time of the post-test that they would be willing to participate in further research were recontacted and offered a payment of $10 for completion of an additional questionnaire. Due to the inability to locate a number of individuals who changed residence during the period following the initial testing, and to some refusals and non-completions, 76 experimental subjects and 46 nominees were included in the follow-up.

LGAT Outcome Measures

Since the outcomes described by LGAT organizers are neither specific nor easily measurable, selecting appropriate assessment instruments is a major difficulty in LGAT outcome research. Part of the problem arises from the fact that LGAT goals are often phrased in a vague and general manner. For example, Lifespring considers itself "a context in which the ability to experience and express self is transformed so that life is alive, purposeful and complete" (Lifespring, 1985), and the Forum promises to "produce an extraordinary advantage in your personal effectiveness and a decisive edge in your ability to achieve" (Werner Erhard & Associates, 1988). It is not readily clear what psychological measures would correspond to such goals. In addition, some LGAT proponents argue that it may be impossible to assess LGAT outcomes adequately using psychological constructs. With regard to *est*, the philosopher W. W. Bartley commented on this problem, in response to the Ornstein et al. (1975) and the Tondow et al. (1973) studies:

> While results such as these are interesting, they are not entirely to the point, for the terms in which the independent investigators were working are different from *est*'s own terms. *est* does not claim to produce changes in self-image or in health; it aims to enable a *transformation* in one's ability to experience living. It may be difficult to measure this: as Werner himself put it, "The real value of *est* is found in the transformation of the quality of graduates' experience, which is difficult, if not impossible, to measure in the commonplace scientific sense." (1978, p. 262).

---

[4]It can be observed that refusals to participate occurred in somewhat different ways for experimental (i.e., Forum) subjects and nominees. The rate of direct refusals (by mail or phone) was greater for the experimental group than the nominees. On the other hand, nominees, more than experimental subjects, tended to refuse to participate indirectly by not returning the first questionnaire. Nevertheless, as will be discussed later, Forum participants and nominees who completed the first questionnaire were quite similar.

Nevertheless, in order to perform psychological research, one has no choice but to translate proposed LGAT outcomes into measurable psychological constructs.

Before selecting the dimensions to be included in the present outcome questionnaire, hypotheses were generated about which characteristics were most likely to be influenced by Forum involvement. Input was solicited from social and clinical psychologists, Forum leaders and staff members, and people who had past experience with programs like the Forum. The existing LGAT literature also provided information regarding relevant dimensions to assess in this study. The consensus which emerged was to assess the effect of Forum participation on psychological and physical health, the ability to function in day-to-day life and socially, and on philosophical orientation towards life. Eight general domains were selected to tap these dimensions: the experience of positive and negative affective states, self-esteem, social functioning, health, life satisfaction, perceived control, and daily coping. In response to concerns in the literature about psychiatric hazards associated with LGAT participation, measures of psychological symptomatology were also included. Finally, several additional measures of possible relevance to Forum outcome were added to the assessment battery.

The next step was to choose the most appropriate standardized measures of these constructs from the extant literature. An important consideration was to include measures that could assess outcome at short- and long-term intervals. It was hypothesized that some dimensions (e.g., self-esteem) would be more likely to show change at the four-week post-training test interval, but that others (e.g., social network density) would be more likely to show change at the follow-up testing interval. The following measures were included in the questionnaire packet, which is reproduced in Appendix A.

Measures of Positive and Negative Affective States

These variables reflect the frequency and intensity of different affective states, and include measures of both positive and negative affect. Since an implicit objective of the Forum is to change peoples' reactions toward their affective states and to create more adaptive methods of appraising life events, it was hypothesized that, following Forum participation, subjects would experience more positive and less negative affect. The following measures were chosen to tap these outcomes.

The *Affects Balance Scale* (ABS) (Derogatis, 1975) provides a measure of an individual's emotional experience. Respondents indicated to what degree (from "never" to "always" on a five-point Likert scale) they had experienced each of 40 different emotions during the previous week. The scale assesses four specific positive emotions (vigor, joy, contentment, affection), four negative emotions (anger, depression, hostility, guilt), and yields separate scores for the experience of positive and negative emotions as well as a total score (the difference between the positive and negative scores). Normative data for the ABS (Derogatis, 1975) were available for the general population and for individuals undergoing a stressful life event (Derogatis, Abeloff, & Melisaratos, 1979), and satisfactory reliability and validity have been obtained. Internal consistency for this measure was .92 in a pilot study performed by our research team.

The *Intensity-Duration Index* was constructed to measure the intensity and duration of self-reported emotional states over time. The emotional states queried were taken from the ABS. Four positive and four negative emotions were included, and subjects indicated how strongly they experienced each in the past week (intensity) and for how long (duration), on a five-point Likert scale. The inclusion of the Intensity-Duration Index allowed for assessment of change in intensity and duration of self-reported emotional states over time, and reflected an important global measure of the quality of emotional experience (see Diener, Larsen, Levine, & Emmons, 1985). Internal consistencies for the intensity and duration measures were calculated separately for each scale and for positive and negative emotions. The average of the four alphas was .70.

Self-Esteem

Prior research has suggested that LGAT participation may result in increased self-acceptance (Hazen, 1980; Weiss, 1977) and improved self-image (Tondow et al., 1973). These might be viewed as corollaries of the increased personal effectiveness and accomplishment that are among the purported benefits of the Forum.

The *Self-Esteem Inventory* (SEI) (Rosenberg, 1965) measures an individual's attitude toward his or her own self-worth. It has been widely used in research on self-concept, and contains ten statements about the self to which the subject responds using a four-point Likert scale ranging from "strongly disagree" to "strongly agree." The Rosenberg SEI had an alpha of .87 in our pilot study. Detailed discussions of its reliability and validity appear in Robinson and Shaver (1973) and Wylie (1974).

Social Functioning

This variable focused on an individual's interpersonal relationships. It was included to determine whether or not, following participation in the Forum, subjects would be more satisfied with and more effective in their social functioning. As a result of LGAT participation, it was also possible that people's social networks would come to include more individuals who had participated in the LGAT experience.

The *Norbeck Social Support Questionnaire* (NSSQ) (Norbeck, Lindsey, & Carrieri, 1981, 1983) comprised an extensive measure of social support. The reliability and validity of this instrument have been described in Norbeck et al.

(1981, 1983). Respondents completed the NSSQ by listing up to 24 people who were important to them and indicated the length of the acquaintanceship, the frequency of contact, and the degree of satisfaction with the relationship. For each network member listed, three areas of support were assessed. *Emotional support* was defined as the degree to which the respondent felt loved and liked by a particular member of his or her network. *Affiliative support* was the degree to which he or she felt that another could be confided in and could provide affiliative support. Finally, *material support* involved perceptions regarding the availability of small loans, rides, and aid if bedridden. Subjects indicated the level of support perceived in each of these areas for all of the individuals listed, using five-point Likert scales. The sum of the three subscales, an aggregate score of *total network functioning*, provided an overall score of the supportive functioning of the social network.

Due to several questions which were added to the NSSQ by our research team, it was also possible to derive a score representing how much *reciprocity* respondents experienced with their social network. This was derived by asking respondents to assess how much they loved and respected each person they listed, and how much they felt that person loved and respected them. The difference between the means of emotional support received and emotional support felt toward others provided a reciprocity score. Lack of reciprocity was indicated by a larger number (i.e., a larger discrepancy).

The *Social Density Scale*, adapted from Hirsch's Social Network Questionnaire (1979), measured the level of interaction among the people in the subject's network. The subject was asked to list on the horizontal and vertical axes of a matrix the initials of 15 significant others with whom he or she was likely to interact during any one-week period. The subject was then asked to mark an "x" in every box that acted as an intersection of two people who also interacted with each other at least once every week. The more interactions within the social network, the more dense the network. For a discussion of the validity of this scale, see Hirsch (1979, 1980).

This measure was used to assess whether or not subjects with low-density social networks were more likely to be attracted to the Forum. Also, it was hypothesized that the long-term outcome of Forum participation could be related to whether or not the participant formed a new high-density social network that included other Forum participants after the LGAT experience.

Health

This variable was included on the basis of prior findings suggesting health improvements following LGAT participation (Ornstein et al., 1975). Although the Forum does not make any specific claims concerning health effects, one of its exercises deals with eliminating headaches and another deals with sleep problems.

The *General Health Measure* was a 26-item instrument, adapted from Wortman and Silver (1981), and devised for the current study to ascertain the functional health of respondents. Besides assessing the frequency of utilizing medical professionals, the measure asked people to rate their health compared to others and provided an index of the amount of restriction in activity they had experienced due to physical health. Internal consistency for this scale in the pilot study was .75.

The *Report of Sleep Quality* was a measure that asked subjects, on a five-point Likert scale (ranging from "never" to "always"), about their frequency of sleep disruption. Internal consistency for this scale in the pilot study was .80.

Life Satisfaction

One of the major outcomes purported to occur following LGAT participation is an increase in life satisfaction; therefore, such an effect was hypothesized. There were two reasons for this hypothesis: (1) if, as LGAT proponents assert, LGAT participation leads to enhanced functioning in various life domains, this should be accompanied by an increased overall sense of life satisfaction, (2) LGATs purport that one of the outcomes of participation is a shift in the participant's *attitude* toward life satisfaction. Satisfaction is no longer conceived as something contingent upon external circumstances, but rather as a natural condition of well-being. For these reasons, it was hypothesized that ratings of life satisfaction might become more positive after LGAT participation.

The *Satisfaction with Life Scale* was designed to measure subjects' satisfaction with various life domains. It contained a list of 15 life aspects ("My love relationship or marriage," "My degree of recognition or success," "My financial situation," "My sex life," etc.) and a general consideration of "My life as a whole." Responses to each of these items were scored on a seven-point scale (ranging from "delighted" to "terrible") or as "not applicable." This response scale was based on a shorter scale developed and validated by Andrews and Crandall (1976) to measure self-reported well-being. Internal consistency for this scale in the pilot study was .90.

Perceived Control

Several measures of perceived control were included to tap changes in philosophical orientation toward life that might result from participation in the Forum. One of the major Forum themes is that people's outcomes in life are due to their own actions. Thus, the Forum maintains that neither external circumstances nor deterministic powers are responsible for events, nor are they the product of any inner, uncontrollable forces such as "personality," "drives," or "impulses". Therefore, a possible Forum outcome would be an increased perception of control over different aspects of life, such as daily events, health, and happiness. Despite the centrality of the personal responsibility theme in most LGATs, this variable has rarely been studied in LGAT outcome studies.

The *Internal-External Locus of Control Scale* (I-E scale) (Rotter, 1966) was employed as a general measure of locus of control. In this instrument, the factor that accounts for most of the variance is subjects' beliefs about whether rewards (reinforcements) are under their control or controlled by powerful others (Robinson & Shaver, 1973). As an individual trait measure, the I-E scale has been correlated with a broad range of constructs and administered to a variety of populations (Joe, 1971). The internal consistency coefficient from a sample of 400 college students was .70 (Rotter, 1966). It was hypothesized that taking the Forum training should result in a more internal score on the I-E scale (Rotter, 1966).

After careful consideration and consultation with Rotter, the standard I-E measure was shortened. This was done in response to concern over possible reactivity to a 29-item forced-choice scale embedded in a large packet of other measures. The shortened scale contained 14 forced-choice pairs, retaining the format of the original instrument. Internal consistency for the pilot sample, similar to the one reported by Rotter, averaged .70.

The *Health Locus of Control Scale* (Wallston, Wallston, Kaplan, & Maides, 1976) examined individuals' beliefs concerning who controls the state of their health: themselves or an outside force. Its reliability and validity are discussed in Wallston et al. (1976). This scale compliments the I-E scale by measuring locus of control for the domain of health. As Rotter (1966) has noted, specific expectancies for a particular domain are more closely linked to actual behavior than more generalized expectancies. The Health Locus of Control scale was considered an important adjunct to the widely used I-E scale and allowed the assessment of both broad changes in philosophical orientation through the control of outcomes, and changes more closely linked to health behavior. Subjects responded to the 11-item instrument using a six-point Likert scale ranging from "strongly agree" to "strongly disagree." Cronbach's alpha from the pilot study was .74.

Daily Coping

This construct includes the subject's appraisal of various everyday problems and his or her ability to cope with them. It also focuses on the perception of the work place (or whatever occupies the subject during the day) as a source of tensions, conflicts, and pleasant experiences. It was anticipated that following Forum participation, subjects might experience fewer problems and pressures and feel more competent to deal with such events.

The *Daily Hassles Index* (Wortman & Silver, 1981) was a seven-item scale which examined the frequency of minor negative events (i.e., hassles) as well as minor positive events occurring in the subject's life. Subjects indicated on a five-point Likert scale how often each of these types of events had occurred in the last week, how much they were affected by them, and how much control they felt they had over them. Chronbach's alpha was .90 for the three negative items; .76 for the two positive items; and .86 for the two control items.

The *Perceived Occupational Stress Scale* (House, McMichael, Wells, Kaplan, & Landerman, 1979) is a 20-item instrument which provides information about people's feelings and attitudes toward their work. In order to use this measure with the current population, it was modified also to allow homemakers and students to respond. The major domains covered by the instrument are work satisfaction, job stress, conflict, and intrinsic motivation. Four- and five-point Likert scales were used to tap responses to items. In pilot work, the internal consistency for the subscales used averaged .78 and ranged from .60 to .90.

Psychological Symptomatology

This variable focused on different elements of psychological symptomatology. It was included on the basis of the conflicting views, reviewed earlier, regarding the impact of LGAT on psychopathology. The current research is the first LGAT outcome study to assess this issue using an appropriate experimental design.

The *Brief Symptom Inventory* (BSI) (Derogatis & Melisaratos, 1983) has been validated as a fully adequate substitute for the widely-used SCL-90 (Derogatis, 1977).[5] The BSI provides a measure of an individual's subjective distress by obtaining a report (using a five-point Likert scale from "not at all" to "extremely") of how much, in the past week, the individual had been distressed by various symptoms. The instrument generates a General Severity Index (GSI), which combines information on the number of symptoms mentioned by the subject and the intensity of perceived distress. It is the score of primary interest for a non-clinical population (see Derogatis & Melisaratos, 1983).

Psychological symptomatology as measured by the BSI was divided into three separate constructs for the present research: psychological symptomatology A (depression and hostility), psychological symptomatology B (anxiety, obsessive compulsiveness and phobic anxiety) and psychological symptomatology C (psychoticism and paranoid ideation). This division was corroborated by a confirmatory factor analysis.

---

[5]Short forms of this instrument and others were employed, when possible, to reduce the possibility of fatigue or adverse reaction due to the length of the questionnaire.

Other Measures

Several other measures relevant to Forum outcome were included. We will discuss each of them below.

Many LGATs, such as the Forum, place a premium on self-awareness at least as an intermediate step toward achieving the goals of the intervention. The *Self-Consciousness Scale* (SCS) (Feningstein, Scheier, & Buss, 1975), which measures self-awareness, is valuable for assessing the degree to which Forum participants become more aware of inner thoughts and feelings, particularly in the short-run. It consists of 23 items which a principle components analysis revealed to be comprised of three distinct factors, making up the three subscales of the SCS (Feningstein et al., 1975). Private self-consciousness reflects the degree to which a person attends to inner thoughts and feelings. Public self-consciousness refers to an awareness of the self as a social being capable of having an impact on others. The third factor, social anxiety, involves the experience of uncomfortable feelings around other people.

Completion of the SCS involved subjects' responding to items using a five-point Likert scale ranging from "very like me" to "very unlike me". Test-retest correlations have been reported as follows: private self-consciousness .79; public self-consciousness .84; and social anxiety .73 (Feningstein et al., 1975). Cronbach's alphas in the pilot study for the three scales were: private self-consciousness, .75; public self-consciousness, .81; and social anxiety, .78.

The *Attitudes Toward Self-Improvement Scale* (ASIS) was a 10-item scale designed by the research team to measure how strongly people believe in the utility of achieving self-awareness and in solving problems through participation in activities designed to enhance self-awareness. It utilized a four-point Likert scale ranging from "very unlike me" to "very much like me," with no mid-point. Among the items were: "I feel there is a deeper meaning in life to be found" and "I am the type who usually takes care of problems myself". High scores on this scale would be more likely to reflect a world view that includes participation in activities like the Forum than would low scores. This instrument might also predict who would continue to participate in Forum-related activities following initial Forum participation. The average Cronbach's alpha for pre- and post-tests was above .80. Test-retest reliability for tests administered 7 weeks apart was .78.

The *Life Events Scale* (LES) was devised by Sarason, Johnson, and Siegel (1978) to assess subjects' life changes and their subjective impact at the time of the event. The original instrument included a list of 47 common events, both positive and negative (e.g., marriage, death of a close family member, changes in work situation). In the present research, subjects were asked to indicate those events they had experienced in the past year and in the past five years and to evaluate the impact on them at the time they occurred. Impact ratings were made on a seven-point bipolar scale, ranging from extremely negative (-3) to extremely positive

(+3). Test-retest reliability for the scale was found to be .63 (Sarason et al., 1978).

The current study added an additional "impact now" measure, which requested that subjects rate the present impact of each event on them. Inclusion of this variable allowed the investigation of the relation between the continuing impact of certain life events and participation in LGAT. Fenwick (1976) speculated that LGAT participation is frequently associated with prior negative life events (e.g., romantic separation, rejection, academic dropout, etc.) that are as yet unresolved for the individual. This modification of the LES enabled the researchers to test the validity of such a speculation. In addition, the modified LES allowed the assessment of the effect of Forum participation on the subsequent experience of these events. One of the Forum themes is that the meaning of past events is under the choice of the individual, and a consequence of this might be the cognitive reframing of past events so that they appear to be less negative.

The *Marlowe-Crowne Social Desirability Index* (Crowne & Marlowe, 1960) constitutes a method of measuring an individual's motivation to "look good" to those in authority. In addition, it could assess pre- to post-Forum changes in subjects' tendency to endorse socially approved views as opposed to their own. The present study modified the Marlowe-Crowne Social Desirability Index (Crowne & Marlowe, 1960), reducing the total number of items from 33 to 12. The final items were carefully selected, paying particular attention to preservation of the original dimensions which Crowne and Marlowe (1960) constructed. The average Cronbach's alpha of the short form for pre- and post-tests was .70.

At the end of the questionnaire, *demographic information* was requested (e.g., the number of people living in the subject's household, religious preference, the importance of religion to the subject, race, sexual preference, occupation, annual income, and education). A shortened version of these questions was also included in the follow-up study.

Measures Included Only in the Follow-Up Study

All the measures described above were included in the pre- and post-testing and were repeated in the follow-up study. In addition, several new measures were added for the follow-up testing (see Appendix A). These reflected two major categories—*descriptive measures* and *measures of expectancies*.

Descriptive Measures

The descriptive measures were included to gain information about events, relationship changes, and involvements that might have occurred in participants' lives after Forum participation. These measures included an index of significant events, a relational change index, and an index of subjects' involvement with organized non-work-related activities.

Significant events index. Subjects were asked to describe briefly three major life events which occurred during the past year that had special significance for them (e.g., personal achievements or disappointments) and to attribute their occurrence to one of six reasons: acquired ability, acquired knowledge, the actions of others, joint efforts of self and others, luck, and God's will. Participants were also asked to explain the significance of each event for them.

Relational change index. Subjects were requested to list the initials of friends or family members with whom they had experienced a major relationship change (either increased or decreased closeness) during the past year. They were asked to indicate the person's relationship to them (e.g., spouse, sister, friend) and the reason for the change. These reasons were divided into three categories: those related primarily to the subject (e.g., "I liked the way I felt around this person"), those related to the other person (e.g., "He/she was someone I could respect") or those related primarily to the relationship (e.g.,"The relationship was becoming more satisfying").

Degree of involvement questionnaire. Subjects were instructed to indicate the name of an organized, non-work related activity (e.g., the Elks, the Sierra Club) with which they had been involved during the previous year. In addition, they were specifically requested to report on any growth-oriented activities (e.g., TM, the Forum, Lifespring) in which they had been involved. There were also questions about the perceived costs and benefits associated with each activity, the amount of time spent on it, the specific nature of the involvement, the perceived importance of the activity, and the participation of friends and family members in it.

Measures of Expectancies

In addition to the above descriptive measures, several measures of expectancies were added for the follow-up testing. The measures of expectancy assessed subjects' beliefs about their abilities to attain success in certain domains, and to undergo positive personal changes.

Expectation for success scale. The expectation for success scale (Fibel & Hale, 1978) was devised to measure generalized expectancies for success in a variety of situations and domains (e.g., goal attainment, carrying out responsibilities). The original scale consisted of 30 items, but only the first 10, which related to general efficacy, were included in the present study. Responses were elicited on a five-point Likert scale.

Private conceptions about change (PCAC). The PCAC is part of a larger instrument still under development (Klar & Nadler, 1988) that assesses the expectations people have about the occurrence of personal change in their lives. The PCAC consists of 13 pairs of adjectives describing peoples' attitudes about significant changes. Subjects indicated their response to each pair of adjectives on a seven-point, semantic differential scale. There were also six additional items, on which subjects expressed their agreement or disagreement with statements about the nature of change (e.g., once significant change is achieved in one area, subsequent change is likely to follow with greater ease).

Chapter III
Results

Preliminary Analyses

Profile of Subjects in the Forum and Peer-Nominee Groups

Demographic Characteristics. Table 3.1 presents the demographic characteristics of the Forum participants in the study, and of the peer nominee control group. As can be seen in the table, there is overall similarity on demographic dimensions between Forum participants and nominee controls. Both samples are highly

---

Table 3.1. Demographic Characteristics of Forum Participants and Nominees

	Forum (n = 135)	Nominee (n = 73)
Gender		
Male	40.0%	31.5%
Female	60.0%	68.5%
Years of Education	15.0%	14.9%
Sexual Preference		
Heterosexual	92.5%	94.4%
Homosexual	6.8%	2.8%
Bisexual	0.8%	2.8%
Race		
White	91.7%	97.2%
Black	3.0%	2.8%
Hispanic	2.3%	0.0%
Asian	1.5%	0.0%
Other	1.5%	0.0%

continued on next page

Table 3.1. continued	Forum	Nominee
Religion		
Protestant	21.6%	24.7%
Jewish	6.7%	12.3%
Catholic	26.9%	38.4%
Other	11.9%	12.3%
None	32.8%	12.3%
Importance of Religion		
Not at all important	18.8%	9.6%
Not too important	35.3%	28.8%
Fairly important	22.6%	30.1%
Very important	14.3%	16.4%
Extremely important	9.0%	15.1%
Attendence at Religious Services		
Never	16.4%	15.3%
Rarely	62.7%	50.0%
Once or twice a month	9.7%	11.1%
Once a week	7.5%	16.7%
More than once a week	3.7%	6.9%
Annual Income - Self Only		
Under 8,000	14.5%	19.4%
8,000 - 12,000	16.0%	6.0%
12,000 - 20,000	31.3%	34.3%
20,000 - 30,000	21.4%	25.4%
30,000 - 50,000	14.5%	10.4%
50,000 - 75,000	0.0%	4.5%
More than 75,000	2.3%	0.0%
Annual Income - Family		
Under 8,000	4.6%	1.5%
8,000 - 12,000	9.9%	4.5%
12,000 - 20,000	18.3%	16.7%
20,000 - 30,000	17.6%	31.8%
30,000 - 50,000	27.5%	22.7%
50,000 - 75,000	11.5%	13.6%
More than 75,000	10.7%	9.1%

continued on next page

Table 3.1. continued	Forum	Nominee
Living Alone		
Yes	19.7%	12.3%
No	80.3%	87.7%

educated, predominantly heterosexual and white. There was only one significant difference between the two groups on the demographics measured: Forum participants were more likely than nominees to report "none" under "religious preference," X^2 (4, N = 208) = 11.68, $p < .02$.

Psychological comparability. To assess the initial *psychological* comparability between the peer nominee control group and Forum participants pre-intervention, multivariate comparisons were performed on the 11 major outcome dimensions represented in the study. (The process by which these outcome dimensions were derived from the measures included in the research is discussed below.) Of the 11 constructs, there was significant pre-Forum nonequivalence between Forum participants and the nominee control group on only two— perceived control and daily coping. Forum participants were initially more internal on locus of control and reported more daily hassles, work pressures, and conflicts at work.

In a univariate analysis of 42 additional variables not included in the 11 multivariate constructs, there were only two initial differences between the two groups. Prospective Forum participants were initially more favorable than nominees toward self-awareness and change-oriented activities as measured on the ASIS (Attitudes toward Self-Improvement Scale). In addition, Forum participants, compared to peer-nominees, tended to view past negative life events during the last year as currently having more impact on them. There were no differences in the number of negative events experienced by the two groups in the past year. Given the large number of comparisons that were attempted, the overall psychological comparability between the groups was substantial.[1]

---

[1] In some sense, the more comparable the experimental and control groups initially, the more credence can be given to the assertion that any post-treatment differences are attributable to the treatment rather than to other unknown factors (e.g., those which predisposed Forum participants to self-select into LGAT). However, any initial differences between the two groups can be handled statistically. Structural equation modeling enables estimating the amount of non-equivalence between the Forum sample and the peer nominee control group and controlling for it when evaluating treatment effects.

Effect of Attrition

Another series of comparisons were made between subjects who completed the various stages of the study (i.e., pre-, post-, and follow-up testing) and those who did not on all measures of interest. A series of *t*-tests which compared the pre-tests of the 83 experimental subjects in Group 1 who completed both the pre- and post-tests and those who completed only the pre-test (N = 34) revealed only four significant differences out of 138 comparisons. Parallel analyses between the 73 nominees who completed both sets of questionnaires and those who completed only the pre-test (N = 21) yielded only two significant differences. A similar set of analyses were performed on the post-test scores of the 76 Forum participants who completed both the post-test and the follow-up and those Forum participants who completed the post-test but not the follow-up (N = 58). Out of 83 possible comparisons, only two were significant. Similar analyses revealed no significant differences for the nominees who completed the post-test and the follow-up (N = 46), and those who did not (N = 27). These findings allow the conclusion that attrition both from pre- to post- test and from post-test to follow-up did not change the characteristics of the experimental and the control samples.

Gender Differences

Initial analyses were performed to assess whether the 11 general outcome dimensions were influenced by gender. Fewer differences emerged than would be expected by chance. For this reason, gender will not be discussed further.

Analysis of the Data

There are at least two important features of the present design that were considered when planning the data analysis. First, since the design is quasi-experimental rather than experimental, the estimation of the treatment effect is somewhat complex. The primary complication arises from the utilization of a biased (i.e., non-random) rather than a random rule by which to assign individuals to the treatment (Forum) and comparison (nominee control group) conditions. In order to analyze the data from the present non-equivalent control group design correctly, explicit attention must be given to controlling for the effect of non-random assignment (cf. Campbell & Stanley, 1966).

There have been two traditional univariate analysis strategies for the non-equivalent control group design: the analysis of covariance and the analysis of change scores (Campbell & Stanley, 1966; Judd & Kenny, 1981; Reichardt, 1979). Each type of analysis may yield different results; however, this is to be expected since the implementation of each analysis is based on very different sets of assumptions (Judd & Kenny, 1981; Kenny, 1979).

In the present study, it was assumed that the impact of the assignment variable on criterion measurements (post-test scores) would be mediated by the pre-test measurements and the treatment. Thus, the analysis of covariance (i.e., regression adjustment) strategy was implemented for the estimation of treatment effects (cf. Judd & Kenny, 1981). According to Campbell and Stanley (1966), treating the pre-test measurement as the covariate serves to equalize treatment and comparison groups that, due to non-random assignment to conditions, are assumed to be non-equivalent. The treatment effect can then be assessed over and above any pre-existing group differences. Using an alternative set of assumptions, a regression adjustment strategy would be considered appropriate. Specifically, if it is assumed that the assignment variable has a direct effect on both the pre-test and the criterion and that this effect is equal in magnitude, then the analysis of change scores would be most appropriate.

A second set of issues was considered when the data analysis was undertaken. Again, this was due to individuals self-selecting into the treatment and nominee control groups. Assuming that individuals self-select into existing groups (in this case the treatment and nominee groups) based upon their *true* scores on a measurement (Lord, 1960), "the post-test should be regressed not on the *measured* pre-test as in traditional covariance analysis but on the *true* pre-test" (Kenny, 1975, p. 351; italics in original). Thus, pre-test measurements must be partitioned into a true score component and an error component.

A statistically technical discussion of this problem is presented in Kenny (1975), and a less technical discussion of its implications can be found in Judd and Kenny (1981). Judd and Kenny (1981) maintain that when individuals self-select into conditions of the NECG design, failure to make some adjustment of the pre-test score to correct for unreliability is rarely a defensible analysis strategy. Analysis of covariance *without* correction of the pre-test for unreliability is likely to produce biased estimates of the treatment effect. However, although implementation of the reliability correction strategy will produce univariate estimates of the treatment effect that are less biased, these estimates cannot be tested for statistical significance because they have unknown distributional properties.

Estimation of a reliability coefficient of the pre-test in order to make the correction is also a matter of considerable importance (cf. Reichardt, 1979). When the analysis is univariate rather than multivariate, it is often necessary to utilize an estimate of the internal consistency of the pre-test measure as an index of reliability. A preferable alternative is to use estimates of reliability that are known with a high degree of certainty, although this is rarely feasible. For this reason and others (e.g., inability to test for statistical significance when implementing a reliability correction strategy), univariate analysis of covariance of the NECG design has been criticized on technical grounds (Judd & Kenny, 1981; Kenny, 1975, 1979). The problems associated with the univariate analysis of the NECG design are handled most appropriately by implementing a multivariate analysis strategy (Judd & Kenny, 1981; Kenny, 1975).

In the present study, for the reasons mentioned above, multivariate analysis was employed where possible. However, it was also complimented by a series of parallel univariate analyses. In addition to statistical considerations, the choice of whether to rely primarily on a univariate or a multivariate strategy in a particular case depended on the purpose of the analysis. Multivariate analyses are superior for handling variables which form conceptually related constructs (e.g., assessing the effects of Forum participation on the multiple indicators of social functioning), and were utilized in that context. However, when a very specific dimension was of interest or when it was not possible to construct a meaningful set of items for multivariate analysis, the univariate approach was used. Because the univariate analysis strategy entails making a large number of statistical comparisons and is less sound statistically than the multivariate analysis, interpretations of effects should be made very cautiously.

Experimental Groups Used in the Analyses

Several different types of multivariate and univariate analyses were performed on the data. At the multivariate level, analyses were performed to assess both the short- and long-term effects of Forum participation. All of these involved subjects from Group 1 (Forum participants who completed pre- and post-tests) and Group 3 (nominees who completed pre- and post-tests). Parallel univariate analyses assessed the short- and long-term effects of Forum participation using Groups 1 and 3. While Group 2 subjects (who completed the post-test only) could not be utilized in the above analyses, univariate analyses assessing the interval from the post-test to the follow-up involved Groups 1, 2 and 3. In these, Groups 1 and 2 were collapsed. The statistical rationale for combining them was the finding that of 32 comparisons between the post-test scores of the two groups, only two were statistically significant.[2]

Multivariate Model of the Treatment Effect

As discussed previously, because subjects self-selected into the treatment and control conditions of the non-equivalent control group design, the criterion measure (i.e., the post-test) must be regressed on the latent true score of the assignment variable (i.e., the latent pre-test), rather than on the measured assignment variable as in the traditional analysis of covariance (Kenny, 1975; Lord, 1960). This

---

[2]As mentioned earlier, Group 2 was originally included to test for the possible interaction of treatment and testing. The data analyses revealed no such interaction.

requires the separation of "true" scores from scores including error. To accomplish this, measurement models had to be specified and estimated to indicate each of the latent theoretical constructs which were represented in the outcome measures. These theoretical constructs were determined by clustering together related measures which tapped central dimensions which the Forum was hypothesized to influence. For example, Health Locus of Control, Control over Hassles and Pleasant Events and Locus of Control were used to form an index of the Perceived Control Construct. (See Table 3.2 for a list of the 11 general constructs which resulted, and the variables used to indicate them.) In effect, measured variables thought to be determined by the same conceptual dimension were used simultaneously to form a composite index or scale, which permitted the separation statistically of latent true scores on the index from random error. The separation of true scores from error was accomplished by a confirmatory factor analysis. Across the 11 general constructs, the average factor loading was .71, with loadings across constructs ranging from .61 to .84. This suggests that the indicators adequately assessed the 11 general constructs they were assumed to measure.

Multivariate Analyses of the Short-Term Effects of Forum Participation

Specification of the structural equation models. The short-term structural equation models all shared several common features. First, all of the models included the same three latent variables: the treatment variable, the assignment variable (pre-test), and the criterion variable (post-test). These variables must be included in any analysis of the non-equivalent control group design.

The short-term structural models employed were all three variable, three parameter models, and were thus identified (i.e., there was adequate known information to estimate all of the unknown structural parameters of interest). In all cases, the indicators of the assignment variable and the criterion variable were the pre-test and the post-test scores on a given dimension. (An example of the basic structural equation model is presented in Figure 3.1.) Finally, in all models, the treatment variable was indicated without error, and was binary coded. Specifically, treated subjects were coded 1, and nominees were coded 3.

The structural model considers the true criterion variance to be a function of the true score on the assignment variable plus the effect of treatment, while controlling for the correlation between the treatment and assignment variables. In other words, it assesses whether or not there is a treatment effect after controlling for pre-existing differences between the two groups. In the model, the path (i.e., arrow) from the assignment variable (pre-test) to the criterion variable (post-test) is an index of the stability of the measure from pre- to post-testing (see Figure 3.1). The path from the treatment to the criterion (post-test) is the estimate of the

Table 3.2.   Multivariate Constructs for the Causal Models

Positive Affect Construct
Positive Affects Balance Scale Score
Intensity of Positive Emotions
Duration of Positive Emotions

Negative Affect Construct
Negative Affects Balance Scale Score
Intensity of Negative Emotions
Duration of Negative Emotions

Health Construct
Item from Satisfaction with Life Scale on Health
General Health score
Somatization score from BSI

Psychological Symptomatology Construct A (from BSI)
Depression
Hostility

Psychological Symptomatology Construct B (from BSI)
Anxiety
Obsessive-Compulsiveness
Phobic Anxiety

Psychological Symptomatology Construct C (from BSI)
Psychoticism
Paranoid Ideation

Perceived Control Construct
Control over hassles and pleasant events
Health Locus of Control score
Locus of Control score

Social Functioning Construct
Item from Satisfaction with Life Scale on friends and social life
Satisfaction with Social Support Network
Total Social Functioning score

continued on next page

Table 3.2. continued

Life Satisfaction Construct
Item on Affects Balance Scale about feeling satisfied
Average score on Satisfaction with Life Scale
Item about job satisfaction

Self-Esteem Construct
Item on Affects Balance Scale about feeling worthless
Self-Esteem Inventory score
Esteem at work

Daily Coping Construct
Conflict between work and other areas of life
Coping with hassles
Pressure at work

Note: BSI=Brief Symptom Inventory. Reprinted from Fisher, Silver, Chinsky, Goff, Klar, & Zagieboylo (1989). Copyright 1989 by the American Psychological Association. Reprinted by permission of the publisher.

---

treatment effect. The curved arrow from the assignment variable to the treatment variable indicates the degree of correlation between pre-test measure and group membership (i.e., treatment or nominee group), and is thus an index of the non-equivalence of the two groups prior to treatment.

The stability of latent true scores from pre- to post-testing is estimated by parameter b, while the treatment effect is estimated by parameter a. Parameter a is of prime interest; it estimates the effect of Forum participation. The degree of non-equivalence of the groups on pre-test measurements is reflected by parameter c. Parameter c is necessarily included in the multivariate model to guarantee both precision and adjustment of the estimate of the treatment effect, based on the non-equivalence of the two groups.

In the measurement model, the latent assignment and criterion variables were indicated by at least two measures. All of the measurement models were identified. Measurement model estimates are an indication of how well the measures chosen to represent a given construct actually relate to it.

Estimating the parameters of the short-term structural models. Parameters of the structural models were estimated by analysis of variance-covariance matrices using Jöreskog and Sörbom's (1986) LISREL VI. The analysis of the Positive Affect dimension will be presented in detail. The results of the other 10 conceptual

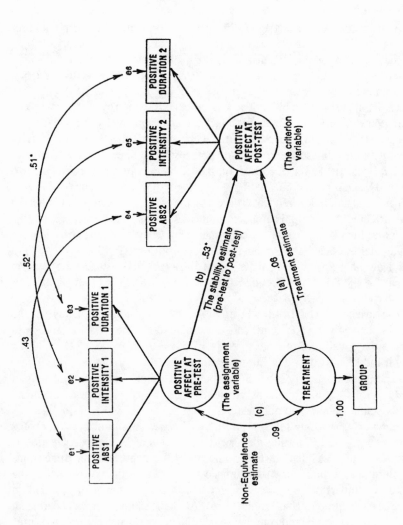

Figure 3.1. A Representative Short Term Structural Model -- The Positive Affect Dimension

dimensions (i.e., Negative Affect, Health, Psychological Symptomatology A, Psychological Symptomatology B, Psychological Symptomatology C, Perceived Control, Social Functioning, Life Satisfaction, Self-Esteem and Daily Coping) will be summarized afterward, since for the most part they yielded the same results as the Positive Affect dimension.

At the outset, consider the specification of the Positive Affect model presented in Figure 3.1. The model has three indicators of the assignment variable (i.e., the latent true score on this dimension), and three indicators of the latent Positive Affect criterion dimension. Treatment is indicated by the binary coded variable, Group, and is assumed to be free of error.

The estimate of the stability of positive affect is provided by parameter b. The standardized structural coefficient for b is .53, and is statistically reliable ($Z(136) = 4.87$, $p < .05$). This indicates that the true score component of the Positive Affect dimension was reliably stable from pre- to post-testing. The estimate of parameter c, which reflects the degree of correlation (i.e., non-equivalence) between the two groups is .09, and is not significant ($Z(136) = .91$, $p > .05$). This implies that Forum participants and nominees were not different on the pre-test measures that indicated positive affect. Parameter a is of greatest interest because it tests the effect of the treatment on the latent Positive Affect dimension. The structural coefficient for this parameter is .06, and is not reliably different from zero ($Z(136) = .76$, $p > .05$). This indicates that participating in the Forum did not result in a difference between the groups on the Positive Affect dimension at the post-test (i.e., four weeks after Forum participation).

The structural model of the Positive Affect dimension adequately fits the data, as indicated by the non-significant chi-square test of the model's capacity to reproduce the covariance matrix, X^2 (9, N = 154) = 9.33, $p > .05$. Overall, the structural model indicates that Forum participation does not have a significant impact upon participants' positive affect, measured a short time after treatment. It also indicates that the measurements on variables that reflect positive affect remain relatively stable from pre- to post-testing.

Summary of the other short-term structural models. A summary of the results of the structural models testing the short-term effects of Forum participation is presented in Table 3.3. Included are estimates of the stability of the dimensions from pre- to post-testing (parameter b), an estimate of the non-equivalence of the treated and comparison groups on the pre-test measures (parameter c), and an estimate of the treatment effect (parameter a). All of the estimates are standardized.

Overall, the results indicate that on all dimensions, true scores (i.e., scores with error removed) remained stable from pre- to post-testing. The stability estimate can be thought of as an over-time estimate of measurement reliability. In addition, on nine out of the 11 constructs, the non-equivalence estimate was not significant. This indicates that prior to treatment, the treatment and nominee groups were quite similar. The two domains in which non-equivalence was observed were

Table 3.3. Summary of the Short-Term Structural Equation Models

Dimension	Stability Estimate(b)	Non-Equivalence Estimate(c)	Treatment Estimate (a)
Positive Affect	.53 *	.09	.06
Negative Affect	.49 *	-.17	.07
Health	.77 *	-.12	.07
Psychological Symptomatology A	.54 *	-.10	.10
Psychological Symptomatology B	.75 *	-.12	.06
Psychological Symptomatology C	.65 *	-.17	-.01
Perceived Control	.84 *	-.26 *	-.19 *
Social Functioning	.61 *	-.17	.07
Life Satisfaction	.76 *	.12	-.01
Self-Esteem	.81 *	-.00	.05
Daily Coping	.75 *	-.29 *	.11

Note: Asterisk indicates a statistically significant estimate ($p < .05$).
Adapted from Fisher et al. (1989). Copyright 1989 by the American Psychological Association. Adapted by permission of the publisher.

for the dimensions of Perceived Control and Daily Coping. The non-equivalence estimates for both of these constructs are negatively signed, suggesting that prior to treatment, Forum participants had a more internal locus of control and were feeling more "hassled" than the nominee group. A significant treatment effect at the .05 level was evident only for the Perceived Control construct. This means that even when controlling for the fact that Forum participants had a more internal locus of control than nominees prior to the Forum, Forum participation strengthened this initial difference. No treatment effect was found on any of the other dimensions, making Perceived Control the only construct exhibiting a short-term treatment effect.

The Short-Term Univariate Analysis of Covariance Model

In addition to the multivariate analyses, parallel univariate analyses of covariance were performed to assess the short-term treatment effects.[3] These analyses incorporated the variables in the 11 conceptual dimensions represented above in the multivariate analyses, as well as the other variables which were included in the study, but not in the above analyses. The univariate model that was estimated for the short-term effects (pre- to post-testing) is:

$$Y = bo + bA + aT + e$$

Variables A and T are the assignment variable (i.e., the pre-test) and the treatment variable, respectively, and Y is the criterion (i.e., the post-test) measurement. The term e is a residual (i.e., error) component in the model. The term bo is the intercept and b can be thought of as a coefficient of stability for a particular dimension (i.e., it is the degree to which the measurements on the dimension remain stable from pre- to post-testing, controlling for the effect of treatment). The coefficient a is the unstandardized estimate of the treatment effect which indexes the impact of Forum participation. It is the parameter of particular interest in the present context. To estimate the parameters of the analysis of covariance model, multiple regression was used.

Parameters of the short-term univariate model. We will first discuss the univariate analysis of the individual variables which comprise the 11 conceptual dimensions represented in the multivariate analysis. Presented in Table 3.4 are stability coefficients (b), unstandardized estimates of the treatment effect (i.e., the parameter a), and the t statistic which tests the null hypothesis that the estimate of parameter a is equal to zero (i.e., that there is no treatment effect).

Examination of the univariate results in Table 3.4 shows that all of the criterion dimensions were stable from pre- to post-test. This means that subjects with low pre-test scores had low post-test scores; that those with high pre-test scores had high post-test scores; and that the rank order from low to high scores stayed approximately the same from pre- to post-test. Further examination of Table 3.4 suggests that of the univariate tests of the treatment effect, there was a reliable effect on four criterion dimensions. For one of these (Coping with Hassles), the estimate of parameter a had a positive weight, indicating that the nominee group mean was significantly higher than the treatment group mean.

---

[3]The results of the univariate analysis of covariance are presented without a reliability correction because in the present context, including the error biases the estimate of the treatment effect in a conservative direction and permits estimates of statistical significance.

Table 3.4. Univariate Summary of the Treatment Effect Pre-Test to Post-Test

	Stability Coefficient (b)	Uncorrected Treatment Parameter Estimate (a)	t	Number of Cases
Positive Affect Construct				
Positive ABS score	.45 *	.23	.51	149
Intensity of positive emotions	.56 *	-.02	-.87	150
Duration of positive emotions	.53 *	.08	1.49	143
Negative Affect Construct				
Negative ABS score	.49 *	.32	.66	138
Intensity of negative emotions	.48 *	.01	.40	151
Duration of negative emotions	.42 *	.09	1.68	122
Health Construct				
Item from Satisfaction with Life Scale on health	.61 *	.01	.25	156
General health score	.47 *	.07	.63	151
Somatization Score from BSI	.45 *	.00	.02	154
Symptomatology Construct A				
Depression	.51 *	-.04	-1.30	154
Hostility	.39 *	.01	.67	154
Symptomatology Construct B				
Anxiety	.62 *	.02	.65	154
Obsessive/compulsiveness	.52 *	.02	.92	153
Phobic anxiety	.56 *	-.00	-.26	154
Symptomatology Construct C				
Psychoticism	.41 *	-.03	-1.42	153
Paranoid ideation	.52 *	.01	.50	154
Perceived Control Construct				
Control over Hassles/ Pleasant Events	.53 *	-.19	-2.30 *	143
Health Locus of Control	.68 *	-1.10	-3.33 *	146
Locus of Control	.64 *	-.32	-2.49 *	143

continued on next page

Table 3.4. continued	Stability	Treatment	t	N
Social Functioning Construct				
Item from Satisfaction with				
Life Scale on social life	.53 *	-.03	-.51	156
Satisfaction with network	.54 *	-.02	-.58	148
Total social functioning score	.53 *	-.11	-1.30	147
Life Satisfaction Construct				
Feeling satisfied (from ABS)	.37 *	.03	.75	156
Average Satisfaction w/Life score	.73 *	.00	.14	156
Satisfaction with job	.61 *	-.00	-.06	149
Self-Esteem Construct				
Feeling worthless (from ABS)	.54 *	-.01	-.15	156
Self-esteem	.77 *	-.13	-.71	153
Esteem at work	.57 *	-.15	-.77	140
Daily Coping Construct				
Work/life conflicts	.69 *	.08	.74	147
Coping with hassles	.38 *	.36	2.42 *	146
Pressure at work	.74 *	.20	1.71	149

Notes: ABS=Affects Balance Scale. An asterisk indicates a statistically significant t value at $p < .05$. The total degrees of freedom differ from variable to variable due to missing data. The total df ranged from 119 to 153. For the analysis, treated subjects were coded as 1 and nominees were coded as 3. When the treatment effect parameter (i.e., parameter a) is *positive*, this means that the nominee group had higher mean scores on the criterion than the treatment group. When parameter a is *negative*, this means that the treatment group had higher mean scores on the criterion than the nominee group.

This implies that following Forum participation, people report fewer hassles and feel less bothered by hassles. The remaining three criterion variables (Control over Hassles and Pleasant Events, Health Locus of Control, and Locus of Control) that showed significant treatment effects had negative values, indicating that the treatment group had higher perceived control than the nominee group. These variables had been included in the Perceived Control construct of the multivariate analyses, and the present findings corroborate the multivariate result that Forum participation increased perceived control.

Of special interest is Table 3.5, which summarizes the univariate analyses for the additional variables that were tested for outcome effects, but that were not part of the 11 multivariate constructs. Most of the variables presented follow the pattern reflected in Table 3.4 of stability over time, and no differences between Forum participants and controls at the post-test. The two exceptions are the measure of the extent to which self-awareness and change-oriented activities are accepted by the individual, and an index of the duration of emotions experienced during the last week. For the first variable, Forum participants were more positive than nominees toward self-awareness and change-oriented activities, t (152) = 3.42, $p < .001$. The duration of emotion variable had a positive weight, indicating that at the post-test, Forum participants experienced particular emotions for a shorter duration of time, t (115) = 2.21, $p < .03$. Due to the large number of tests performed, and the statistical inadequacies associated with the use of univariate analysis of covariance for the NECG design, all of the univariate findings should be viewed cautiously.

Multivariate Analysis of the Long-Term Effects of Forum Participation

A set of multivariate and parallel univariate analyses quite similar to the short-term analyses were performed on the long-term (follow-up) data. It is important to bear in mind that since some individuals either declined to participate in the follow-up study or could not be contacted by mail or phone, the number of subjects in these analyses is reduced. In some of the *univariate* analyses this was compensated for by the fact that members of Group 2 could be included. As noted earlier, this was deemed acceptable since Group 2 was not found to be significantly different from Group 1. However, members of Group 2 could not be included in any of the *multivariate* analyses or in the univariate analyses that involved the pre-test measures.

The structural models: Long-term analysis. The structural models employed to estimate the long-term effects of Forum participation followed the same logic as the short-term structural models. The same 11 conceptual dimensions were used. A representative model of one of the conceptual dimensions, Positive Affect, is presented in Figure 3.2. The model has three indicators of the assignment variable (i.e., the latent true score on this dimension), and three indicators of the latent Positive Affect dimension as measured in the post-test and in the follow-up. The follow-up serves as the criterion variable. Treatment is indicated by the binary coded variable, Group, and is assumed to be free of error. An examination of Figure 3.2 reveals that the Positive Affect dimension is stable both in the short-term (parameter a) and in the long-term (parameter b). There is

Table 3.5. Univariate Summary of the Additional Variables Pre-Test to Post-Test
(Variables not Included in the Multivariate Constructs)

	Stability Coefficient (b)	Uncorrected Treatment Parameter Estimate (a)	t	Number of Cases
Affects Balance Scale				
Intensity of emotions	.54 *	-.00	-.24	149
Duration of emotions	.51 *	.07	2.21 *	118
Joy	.46 *	.14	1.06	153
Contentment	.49 *	-.06	-.45	150
Vigor	.37 *	.10	.70	152
Affection	.54 *	.06	.49	153
Anxiety	.56 *	.21	1.44	146
Depression	.51 *	.07	.43	151
Guilt	.61 *	-.08	-.55	150
Hostility	.40 *	.13	.84	150
ABS difference score	.49 *	-.06	-.08	135
Health Scale				
Sleep quality	.56 *	.03	.22	156
Self-Consciousness Scale				
Private self-consciousness	.69 *	-.40	-1.51	144
Public self-consciousness	.76 *	.09	.53	150
Social anxiety	.71 *	.15	.91	150
Work Scale				
Satisfaction with job	.76 *	-.07	-.76	143
Intrinsic opportunity at work	.69 *	-.01	-.44	143
Mean of 21 job-related questions	.78 *	-.01	-.40	125
Brief Symptom Inventory				
General Severity Index	.47 *	-.01	-.45	152
Marlowe-Crowne Scale				
Social Desirability	.74 *	.05	.50	154

continued on next page

Table 3.5 continued	Stability	Treatment	t	N
Life Events Scale				
No. negative events in last year	-.99 *	-.02	.55	143
No. negative events in last five years	1.00*	.00	.12	156
Impact of events in last year (then)	.46 *	.51	1.44	156
Impact of events in last five years (then)	.52 *	-.24	-.35	156
Impact of events in last year (now)	.30 *	.29	1.15	152
Impact of events in last five years (now)	.32 *	.03	.07	151
Hassles Scale				
Amount of pleasure from pleasant events	.40 *	.02	.30	150
Attitudes Toward Self-Improvement Scale				
Self-awareness	.81 *	-.65	-3.42 *	155
Norbeck Social Support Scale				
Average relationship length	.39 *	.03	.81	148
Total no. of supports lost last year	.18 *	.02	.14	148
No. family members lost last year	.10	.03	.63	148
No. others lost last year	.23 *	.00	.02	151
Amount of support lost last year	.37 *	-.06	-.83	145
No. people seen more than once a week	.57 *	.05	.28	149
Feeling loved/respected, mean	.50 *	-.05	-1.33	148
Confiding in others	.51 *	-.02	-.59	148
Feel others would help you	.48 *	-.05	-1.24	147
Frequency of contact	.64 *	-.44	-.63	148
Discrepancy in love	.11	-.25	-.57	147
Discrepancy in respect	.29 *	.06	.19	148
Discrepancy in love and respect, combined	.36 *	-.10	-.22	147

continued on next page

Table 3.5 continued	Stability	Treatment	t	N
Density Scale				
Density of social network	.78 *	.01	.79	146

Notes: An asterisk indicates a statistically significant t value at $p < .05$. The total degrees of freedom differ from variable to variable due to missing data. The total df range from 80 to 153. For the analysis, treated subjects were coded as 1 and nominees were coded as 3. When the treatment effect parameter (i.e., parameter a) is *positive*, this means that the nominee group had higher mean scores on the criterion than the treatment group. When parameter a is *negative*, this means that the treatment group had higher mean scores on the criterion than the nominee group.

no initial nonequivalence between Forum participants and nominees (parameter c). Most importantly, there is no long-term treatment effect (parameter d).

General summary of the long-term structural models. A summary of the results for each of the 11 conceptual dimensions is presented in Table 3.6. Parameter a estimates the stability of each conceptual dimension from the first measurement (the pre-test) to the second measurement (the post-test). Parameter b estimates the stability of the dimension between the second (post-test) and the third (follow-up) measurements. Parameter c estimates the degree of initial non-comparability (non-equivalence) between the two groups and parameter d estimates the long-term treatment effect.

One might note that two of these parameters (i.e., stability and non-equivalence) had been estimated in the short-term structural models. However, the two corresponding parameters for the long-term models are not necessarily identical for two reasons. First, the samples used for the short- and the long-term models are not equivalent due to post-test, follow-up attrition. Second, even when the same sample is used in two different structural models, the parameter of a particular path will not be identical since by their very nature these parameters are *estimates* of an effect, rather than a precise measure of it. It is important to recognize this when examining the analyses.

As can be observed from Table 3.6, 10 of the 11 dimensions appear to be stable both in the short-term (parameter a) and in the long-term (parameter b). The only dimension that fails to show this pattern of stability is the Social Functioning dimension. Bearing in mind that this dimension is comprised of indicators of satisfaction with social relations, which are inherently somewhat unstable, this is not especially surprising.

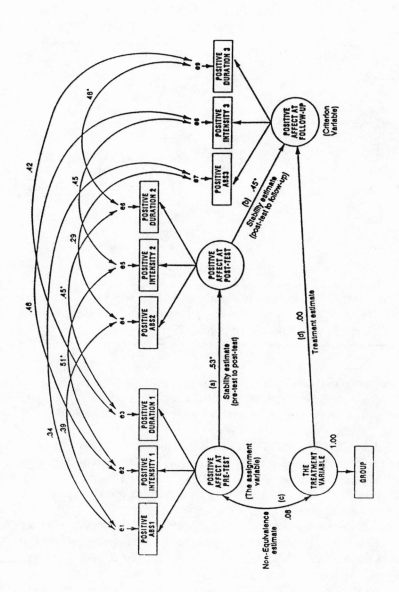

Figure 3.2. A Representative Long Term Structural Model -- The Positive Affect Dimension

Table 3.6. Summary of the Long-Term Structural Equation Models

Dimension	Stability Est. (a)	Stability Est. (b)	Non-Equiv. Est. (c)	Treatment Est. (d)
Positive Affect	.53 *	.45 *	.08	.00
Negative Affect	.64 *	.36 *	-.24	-.09
Health	.82 *	.70 *	-.20	-.03
Psychological Symptomatology A	.66 *	.45 *	-.22 *	-.04
Psychological Symptomatology B	.70 *	.90 *	-.12	-.01
Psychological Symptomatology C	.63 *	.58 *	-.05	-.03
Perceived Control	.97 *	.95 *	-.44 *	-.01
Social Functioning	.61	.48	-.13	-.03
Life Satisfaction	.89 *	.82 *	.10	.04
Self-Esteem	.91 *	.85 *	.02	.09
Daily Coping	.68 *	.68 *	-.09	-.10

Note: Asterisk indicates a statistically significant estimate at $p < .05$. Reprinted from Fisher et al. (1989). Copyright 1989 by the American Psychological Association. Reprinted by permission of the publisher.

In terms of initial non-equivalence between Forum participants and nominees, as was the case for the short-term structural models, the Perceived Control construct appears to reflect non-comparability between the two groups. Another dimension, Psychological Symptomatology A, was significant and suggested noncomparability here as well. The negative sign indicates that Forum participants who participated in the follow-up were initially (i.e., at the pre-test) higher in this type of psychological symptomatology than nominees. On the other hand, the previous non-equivalence on the Daily Coping construct was not replicated in the present set of analyses.

The most important aspect of these analyses involves the parameter for the treatment effect. Inspection of Table 3.6 reveals no significant treatment effect on any of the 11 dimensions. This includes the effect for Perceived Control observed earlier, which has not been replicated in the present analysis. Overall, there appears to be no long-term effect of Forum participation on any of the 11 conceptual dimensions.

The Long-term Univariate Analysis of Covariance Model

In addition to the long-term multivariate analyses, parallel univariate analyses using multiple regression were performed to test for effects from the pre-test to the follow-up testing, and also from post-test to the follow-up testing. It is important to bear in mind that the pre- to follow-up analyses ignore the fact that the post-test occurred, and thus should be interpreted with extreme caution.

Pre- to follow-up analyses. The analysis of covariance model of the effects from the pre-test to the follow-up that was estimated using multiple regression is:

$$Y = bo + bA + aT + e$$

This is the same model as for the short-term analysis, except that the criterion measurement (Y) is now the follow-up test score, instead of the post-test score. Variables A and T are, as before, the assignment variable (i.e., the pre-test) and the treatment variable, respectively. Again, the term e is a residual (i.e., error) component in the model, the term bo is the intercept and b can be thought of as a coefficient of stability for a particular dimension (i.e., it is the degree to which the measurements on the dimension remain stable from pre- to follow-up testing, controlling for the effect of treatment). The coefficient a is the unstandardized estimate of the treatment effect, which indexes the impact of Forum participation.

Parameters of the long-term model: Pre- to follow-up-test. The results of the pre- to follow-up univariate analyses are presented in Table 3.7. Once again, the prevailing pattern is one of significant stability across time and of non-significance of pre- to follow-up differences between Forum participants and nominees. However, there were a number of variables which showed both stability across time as well as significant pre- to follow-up differences.

Two such variables are of particular interest because the data replicate and extend the short-term (pre- to post-test) results discussed earlier. These variables are Control over Hassles and Pleasant Events, and Health Locus of Control. The present results indicate that these treatment effects, as estimated by the long-term *univariate* analyses, persisted for an interval of more than a year. (Recall that these effects were *not* found in the long-term multivariate analyses, which for reasons described earlier, should be given greater weight.) None of the other significant short-term univariate differences discussed earlier (i.e., the effects on duration of affect and attitudes toward self-awareness activities) were paralleled in the pre-to follow-up univariate analysis, perhaps indicating that they were not strong, or that they were short-lived.

Table 3.7 also reveals a few scattered differences between Forum participants and nominees which emerged in the pre-to follow-up analyses, which were *not* present in the short-term univariate analyses. Forum participants had lower social anxiety at the follow-up on the Feningstein et al. (1975) Self-Consciousness

Table 3.7. Univariate Summary of the Treatment Effect Pre-Test to Follow-up

	Stability Coefficient (b)	Uncorrected Treatment Parameter Estimate (a)	t	Number of Cases
Variables included in the Multivariate Constructs				
Positive Affect Construct				
Positive ABS score	.35 *	.51	.63	73
Intensity of positive emotions	.51 *	-.03	-.70	74
Duration of positive emotions	.48 *	-.01	-.18	73
Negative Affect Construct				
Negative ABS score	.36 *	.01	.01	69
Intensity of negative emotions	.16	.04	.90	74
Duration of negative emotions	.26	-.06	-.73	63
Health Construct				
Item from Satisfaction with Life Scale on health	.69 *	-.04	-.52	78
General health score	.40 *	.03	.14	77
Somatization score from BSI	.42 *	.02	.72	78
Symptomatology Construct A				
Depression	.29 *	-.03	-.63	78
Hostility	.20 *	.02	.74	78
Symptomatology Construct B				
Anxiety	.41 *	.02	.48	78
Obsessive/compulsiveness	.46 *	-.01	-.32	77
Phobic anxiety	.59 *	.01	.49	78
Symptomatology Construct C				
Psychoticism	.36 *	-.00	-.05	77
Paranoid ideation	.51 *	-.01	-.39	78
Perceived Control Construct				
Control over Hassles/ Pleasant Events	.46 *	-.26	-2.25 *	71
Health Locus of Control	.70 *	-1.23	-2.52 *	74
Locus of Control	.47 *	-.21	-1.08	72

continued on next page

Table 3.7. continued	Stability	Treatment	t	N
Social Functioning Construct				
Satisfaction with Life Scale				
question on social life	.41 *	-.05	-.62	78
Satisfaction with network	.71 *	-.02	-.47	71
Total social functioning	.64 *	-.12	-1.09	65
Life Satisfaction Construct				
Feeling satisfied (from ABS)	.29 *	.08	1.33	78
Average Satisfaction with Life				
Scale score	.71 *	-.04	-.81	78
Satisfaction with job	.57 *	.00	.04	68
Self-Esteem Construct				
Feeling worthless (from ABS)	.63 *	.06	.98	78
Self-esteem	.81 *	-.28	-1.06	77
Esteem at work	.55 *	.21	.68	65
Daily Coping Construct				
Work/life conflicts	.47 *	.06	.37	69
Coping with hassles	.36 *	-.11	-.57	69
Pressure at work	.36 *	.04	.22	69

Variables Not included in the Multivariate Constructs

	Stability	Treatment	t	N
Affects Balance Scale				
Intensity of emotions	.26 *	.01	.36	73
Duration of emotions	.42 *	.06	-1.06	61
Joy	.25 *	.12	.49	75
Contentment	.28 *	.22	.90	74
Vigor	.46 *	.05	.20	76
Affection	.64 *	-.03	-.14	76
Anxiety	.39 *	.10	.47	71
Depression	.40 *	.08	.29	75
Guilt	.49 *	.00	.02	74
Hostility	.33 *	.01	.04	75
ABS difference score	.35 *	.70	.50	68
Health Scale				
Sleep quality	.63 *	.43	2.26 *	77

continued on next page

Table 3.7. continued	Stability	Treatment	t	N
Self-Consciousness Scale				
Private self-consciousness	.78 *	-.31	-.84	71
Public self-consciousness	.74 *	.30	1.08	74
Social anxiety	.71 *	.55	2.16 *	74
Work Scale				
Satisfaction with job	.64 *	-.25	-1.71	67
Intrinsic opportunity at work	.57 *	-.04	-1.13	69
Mean of 21 job-related questions	.71 *	-.01	-.40	62
Brief Symptom Inventory				
General Severity Index	.46 *	.00	.17	77
Marlowe-Crowne Scale				
Social Desirability	.74 *	.16	.96	76
Life Events Scale				
No. negative events in last year	.19 *	-.57	-.33	72
No. negative events in last five years	.25	.89	-1.66	78
Impact of events in last year (then)	.34 *	-.20	-.20	78
Impact of events in last five years (then)	.40 *	-1.09	-.87	78
Impact of events in last year (now)	.56 *	-.70	-.36	76
Impact of events in last five years (now)	.88 *	-2.46	-.89	76
Hassles Scale				
Amount of pleasure from pleasant events	.16	.02	.19	71
Attitudes Toward Self-Improvement Scale				
Self-awareness	.78 *	-.43	-1.40	78
Density Scale				
Density of social network	.37 *	.01	1.22	73

continued on next page

Table 3.7. continued	Stability	Treatment	t	N
Norbeck Social Support Scale				
Average relationship length	.47 *	.03	.91	72
Total no. of supports lost last year	.14	.14	.43	71
No. family members lost last year	.23 *	-.05	-1.14	72
No. others lost last year	.12	.24	.73	71
Amount of support lost last year	.04	-.08	-.72	71
No. people seen more than once a week	.39 *	.70	2.72 *	76
Feeling loved/respected, mean	.48 *	-.02	-.46	67
Confiding in others	.61 *	-.04	-1.20	71
Feel others would help you	.60 *	-.06	-1.27	72
Frequency of contact	.43 *	-1.15	-1.01	72
Discrepancy in love	.23	-.03	-.10	67
Discrepancy in respect	.30 *	-.02	-.04	66
Discrepancy in love and respect, combined	.36 *	-.19	-.04	66

Notes: An asterisk indicates a statistically significant t value at $p < .05$. The total degrees of freedom differ from variable to variable due to missing data. The total df range from 58 to 75. For the analysis, treated subjects were coded as 1 and nominees were coded as 3. When the treatment effect parameter (i.e., parameter a) is *positive*, this means that the nominee group had higher mean scores on the criterion than the treatment group. When parameter a is *negative*, this means that the treatment group had higher mean scores on the criterion than the nominee group.

Scale, $t (71) = 2.16$, $p < .04$, fewer problems with sleep on the General Health Measure, $t (74) = 2.26$, $p < .03$, and were in contact with fewer people in their social network at least once a week, $t (73) = 2.72$, $p < .01$. However, given the large number of univariate tests attempted, caution should be used in interpreting these effects.

    Parameters of the long-term model: Post- to follow-up analyses. The final set of univariate analyses performed involved the interval from the post- to the follow-up testing. These analyses ignore differences at pre-test and take into account only post-test scores. Thus, they are of interest for assessing treatment effects that either first appeared after the post-testing, or were present at the post-testing and became more pronounced over time. The results of these analyses are presented in Table 3.8.

There was only one variable (control over hassles and pleasant events in one's life) which evidenced a treatment effect in both the pre-post and the pre-follow-up univariate analyses, which remained significant in the post- to follow-up analysis. Juxtaposed with the pre-follow-up univariate finding, the post-follow-up effect suggests an increase in control over hassles and pleasant events from the post- to the follow-up testing.

Only one additional difference evident in the pre- to follow-up analyses was paralleled in the post- to follow-up analyses. This was the observation of a reduction, for Forum participants, in the number of social network members who are in contact with them at least once a week. A final difference that emerged *only* in the post- to follow-up analyses was that Forum participants reported a higher number of negative life events in the last five years. As a whole it should be kept in mind that the dimensions on which the univariate effects occurred, in addition to representing only a very small portion of the variables assessed using univariate techniques, were components of sets of variables measuring particular domains (e.g., social support, impact of life events) that as a whole showed few differences between the two groups. Such scattered findings should not be interpreted as representing reliable effects.

Descriptive Statistics

Presented in Table 3.9 are the means and standard deviations of all the variables that formed the major outcome constructs in the structural equation models. A simple comparison of the mean scores from the pre-, to the post-, to the follow-up testing provides yet another vantage point from which to view the relative "movement" of subjects on the conceptual dimensions over time. Inspection of Table 3.9 suggests the same conclusion as the structural equation models and the univariate analyses, although in a much less refined fashion. Generally, the data in Table 3.9 indicate relatively stable means and standard deviations over time.

Measures Included Only in the Follow-up Study

As was mentioned earlier, some measures were included only in the follow-up study to gain information about aspects of subjects' lives post-Forum. Interpretation of the findings derived from these measures should be made with caution for two reasons. First, they were not included in the pre-test and there is no baseline with which to compare findings, so a confident analysis of treatment effects cannot be made. Second, most of the measures were descriptive in nature

Table 3.8. Univariate Summary of the Treatment Effect Post-Test to Follow-up

	Stability Coefficient (b)	Uncorrected Treatment Parameter Estimate (a)	t	Number of Cases
Variables included in the Multivariate Constructs				
Positive Affect Construct				
Positive ABS score	.36 *	.49	.62	99
Intensity of positive emotions	.37 *	-.03	-.77	102
Duration of positive emotions	.53 *	-.03	-.39	97
Negative Affect Construct				
Negative ABS score	.48 *	-.23	.28	93
Intensity of negative emotions	.36 *	.01	.31	102
Duration of negative emotions	.47 *	-.13	-1.59	89
Health Construct				
Satisfaction with Life				
Item on health	.69 *	-.09	-1.10	105
General health score	.37 *	-.10	-.45	102
Somatization	.33 *	.00	.00	104
Symptomatology Construct A				
Depression	.49 *	-.01	-.22	104
Hostility	.36 *	.02	.61	104
Symptomatology Construct B				
Anxiety	.50 *	-.01	-.17	104
Obsessive/compulsiveness	.55 *	-.02	-.55	104
Phobic anxiety	.53 *	.01	.45	104
Symptomatology Construct C				
Psychoticism	.60 *	.00	.11	104
Paranoid ideation	.52 *	-.01	-.26	104
Perceived Control Construct				
Control over Hassles/				
Pleasant Events	.39 *	-.28	-2.46 *	93
Health Locus of Control	.58 *	-.72	-1.39	101
Locus of Control	.44 *	-.15	-.71	99

continued on next page

Table 3.8. continued	Stability	Treatment	t	N
Social Functioning Construct				
Satisfaction with Life Scale				
Question on social life	.50 *	-.06	-.83	105
Satisfaction with network	.35 *	.03	.68	96
Total social functioning score	.21 *	.06	.54	87
Life Satisfaction Construct				
Feeling satisfied	.27 *	.08	1.29	105
Average Satisfaction with				
Life Scale score	.70 *	-.03	-.70	105
Satisfaction with job	.46 *	-.01	-.28	96
Self-Esteem Construct				
Feeling worthless	.50 *	.04	.66	105
Self-esteem	.76 *	-.13	-.44	103
Esteem at work	.70 *	.30	1.07	92
Daily Coping Construct				
Work/life conflicts	.53 *	-.01	-.07	96
Coping with hassles	.41 *	-.01	-.04	95
Pressure at work	.53 *	-.10	-.66	96

Variables Not included in the Multivariate Constructs

Affects Balance Scale				
Intensity of emotions	.36 *	-.01	-.27	100
Duration of emotions	.46 *	-.08	-1.45	84
Joy	.38 *	.17	.74	102
Contentment	.41 *	.21	.93	101
Vigor	.50 *	.06	.28	102
Affection	.36 *	-.01	-.06	103
Anxiety	.57 *	-.16	-.79	98
Depression	.46 *	-.03	-.10	102
Guilt	.45 *	.01	.03	99
Hostility	.38 *	-.02	-.10	101
ABS difference score	.40 *	.47	.31	90

continued on next page

Table 3.8. continued	Stability	Treatment	t	N
Health Scale				
Sleep quality	.52 *	.35	1.78	105
Self-Consciousness Scale				
Private self-consciousness	.72 *	.07	.20	100
Public self-consciousness	.74 *	.24	.81	102
Social anxiety	.75 *	.43	1.60	102
Work Scale				
Satisfaction with job	.42 *	- .18	-1.13	94
Intrinsic opportunity at work	.61 *	- .05	-1.21	95
Mean of 21 job-related questions	.76 *	- .01	- .46	86
Brief Symptom Inventory				
General Severity Index	.62 *	.00	.09	104
Marlowe-Crowne Scale				
Social Desirability	.59 *	.03	.18	102
Life Events Scale				
No. negative events in last year	.14 *	- .56	-1.45	99
No. negative events in last five years	.19 *	-1.31	-2.49 *	105
Impact of events in last year (then)	.68 *	- .67	- .82	105
Impact of events in last five years (then)	.48 *	-1.35	-1.16	105
Impact of events in last year (now)	.15	- .46	- .28	105
Impact of events in last five years (now)	1.02 *	-2.68	-1.06	103
Hassles Scale				
Amount of pleasure from pleasant events	.36	.02	.23	97
Attitudes toward Self Improvement Scale				
Self-awareness	.77 *	- .25	- .86	102

continued on next page

Table 3.8. continued	Stability	Treatment	t	N
Norbeck Social Support Scale				
Average relationship length	.12	.05	1.35	97
Total no. of supports lost last year	-.01	.14	.47	94
No. family members lost last year	.05	-.05	-1.18	95
No. others lost last year	-.00	.22	.78	96
Amount of support lost last year	-.10	-.05	-.52	97
No. people seen more than once a week	.57 *	.71	2.90 *	101
Feeling loved/respected, mean	.21 *	.03	.62	89
Confiding in others	.26 *	.03	.62	89
Feel others would help you	.33 *	.02	.42	97
Frequency of contact	.53 *	-.52	-.47	97
Discrepancy in love	.28 *	-.19	-.50	90
Discrepancy in respect	.33 *	-.20	-.45	89
Discrepancy in love and respect, combined	.51 *	-.57	-.92	87
Density Scale				
Density of social network	.24 *	.01	.92	97

Notes: An asterisk indicates a statistically significant t value at p <.05. The total degrees of freedom differ from variable to variable due to missing data. The total df range from 81 to 102. For the analysis, treated subjects were coded as 1 and nominees were coded as 3. When the treatment effect parameter (i.e., parameter a) is *positive*, this means that the nominee group had higher mean scores on the criterion than the treatment group. When parameter a is *negative*, this means that the treatment group had higher mean scores on the criterion than the nominee group.

and are not well validated compared to the other instruments employed in the study.

The *significant events measure*. On this measure, subjects could indicate up to three significant events that occurred during the past year. The content of the events were judged by two independent judges and inter-rater reliability was .92. Since the subjects varied in the number of events they reported, initially only the first event subjects recorded was considered. The data indicated that Forum participants

Table 3.9. Descriptive Statistics on the Construct Indicators

| | Participants | | Nominees | |
	Mean	S.D.	Mean	S.D.
POSITIVE AFFECT DIMENSION				
Positive ABS				
Pre-test	49.56	9.99	51.68	8.73
Post-test	50.04	9.61	51.68	8.58
Follow-up	47.48	10.09	49.71	11.09
Intensity				
Pre-test	2.35	.56	2.38	.51
Post-test	2.48	.54	2.43	.66
Follow-up	2.32	.47	2.24	.71
Duration				
Pre-test	3.76	1.14	3.85	1.04
Post-test	3.57	1.12	3.86	1.10
Follow-up	3.60	1.25	3.42	1.19
NEGATIVE AFFECT DIMENSION				
Negative ABS				
Pre-test	25.15	10.36	22.43	9.39
Post-test	20.58	10.25	20.20	9.23
Follow-up	23.57	9.54	23.00	11.32
Intensity				
Pre-test	1.37	.69	1.22	.55
Post-test	1.10	.70	1.06	.61
Follow-up	1.16	.50	1.27	.71
Duration				
Pre-test	1.94	.93	1.84	.90
Post-test	1.50	1.02	1.73	.94
Follow-up	1.68	.93	1.68	.98

continued on next page

Table 3.9. continued	(P) Mean	(P) S.D.	(N) Mean	(N) S.D.
HEALTH DIMENSION				
Satisfaction with Life Item on Health				
Pre-test	1.73	1.12	1.56	1.22
Post-test	1.65	.99	1.58	1.08
Follow-up	1.86	1.40	1.62	1.13
General Health				
Pre-test	2.49	2.97	1.82	2.20
Post-test	2.05	2.37	1.95	2.46
Follow-up	2.74	3.58	2.43	2.84
Somatization				
Pre-test	.33	.45	.25	.44
Post-test	.29	.36	.26	.37
Follow-up	.30	.29	.28	.44
PSYCHOLOGICAL SYMPTOMATOLOGY DIMENSION A				
Depression				
Pre-test	.87	.76	.70	.67
Post-test	.67	.71	.48	.50
Follow-up	.71	.56	.55	.59
Hostility				
Pre-test	.56	.52	.44	.45
Post-test	.41	.43	.41	.45
Follow-up	.41	.29	.45	.45
PSYCHOLOGICAL SYMPTOMATOLOGY DIMENSION B				
Anxiety				
Pre-test	.78	.57	.69	.51
Post-test	.59	.57	.59	.57
Follow-up	.64	.50	.65	.57
Obsessive/Compulsiveness				
Pre-test	1.06	.77	.84	.62
Post-test	.83	.62	.78	.55
Follow-up	.93	.46	.79	.68

continued on next page

Table 3.9. continued	(P) Mean	(P) S.D.	(N) Mean	(N) S.D.
Phobic Anxiety				
Pre-test	.29	.30	.28	.38
Post-test	.27	.29	.28	.39
Follow-up	.28	.27	.27	.48

PSYCHOLOGICAL SYMPTOMATOLOGY DIMENSION C

Psychoticism				
Pre-test	.61	.63	.52	.58
Post-test	.45	.52	.32	.40
Follow-up	.46	.46	.40	.56
Paranoid Ideation				
Pre-test	.76	.66	.58	.48
Post-test	.53	.53	.47	.46
Follow-up	.63	.51	.52	.59

PERCEIVED CONTROL DIMENSION

Control Over Hassles/Pleasant Events				
Pre-test	7.33	1.60	7.22	1.67
Post-test	6.93	1.75	7.31	1.63
Follow-up	7.88	1.61	6.80	1.56
Health Locus of Control				
Pre-test	50.17	6.58	46.36	7.98
Post-test	50.80	6.62	44.91	8.53
Follow-up	51.77	7.56	45.46	8.35
Locus of Control				
Pre-test	9.22	2.86	8.59	2.84
Post-test	10.40	2.77	9.03	3.09
Follow-up	9.92	2.95	8.85	2.88

SOCIAL FUNCTIONING DIMENSION

Satisfaction with Life Scale Item on Social Life				
Pre-test	2.41	1.31	1.88	1.13
Post-test	2.30	1.12	1.95	1.13
Follow-up	2.22	.99	1.93	1.11

continued on next page

Table 3.9. continued	(P) Mean	(P) S.D.	(N) Mean	(N) S.D.
Satisfaction With Network				
Pre-test	3.79	.89	4.02	.53
Post-test	3.89	.72	3.95	.90
Follow-up	3.96	.64	4.06	.63
Total Social Functioning Score				
Pre-test	12.24	1.70	12.34	1.44
Post-test	12.43	1.43	12.15	2.11
Follow-up	12.33	1.60	12.49	1.70

LIFE SATISFACTION DIMENSION

Feeling Satisfied				
Pre-test	2.28	.94	2.36	.63
Post-test	2.41	.78	2.52	.69
Follow-up	2.55	.83	2.55	.83
Average Satisfaction with Life Scale Score				
Pre-test	2.34	.82	2.18	.76
Post-test	2.26	.82	2.15	.78
Follow-up	2.28	.83	2.12	.89
Satisfaction with Job				
Pre-test	1.28	.69	1.40	.57
Post-test	1.34	.66	1.41	.60
Follow-up	1.25	.72	1.33	.58

SELF-ESTEEM DIMENSION

Feeling Worthless				
Pre-test	.58	.78	.49	.84
Post-test	.54	.82	.48	.78
Follow-up	.53	.94	.60	.96
Self-Esteem				
Pre-test	33.38	5.07	33.64	5.13
Post-test	34.14	5.26	33.96	5.06
Follow-up	33.44	5.92	32.85	5.35

continued on next page

Table 3.9. continued	(P) Mean	(P) S.D.	(N) Mean	(N) S.D.
Job Esteem				
Pre-test	12.26	3.72	12.69	4.02
Post-test	34.14	5.26	33.96	5.06
Follow-up	33.44	5.92	32.85	5.35
DAILY COPING DIMENSION				
Work/Life Conflicts				
Pre-test	4.25	2.62	3.44	2.39
Post-test	3.80	2.74	3.49	2.46
Follow-up	3.88	2.03	3.77	2.52
Coping With Hassles				
Pre-test	7.47	2.71	6.52	2.44
Post-test	5.53	3.02	6.26	2.56
Follow-up	7.03	2.64	6.93	2.55
Pressure at Work				
Pre-test	4.97	2.39	4.08	2.58
Post-test	4.72	2.81	4.66	2.74
Follow-up	5.12	2.37	4.97	2.31

reported a higher proportion of positive events than nominees (78.8% of all events mentioned vs. 56%), X^2 (1, N = 122) = 6.92, $p < .05$, and fewer negative events (12.7% vs. 32%), X^2 (1, N = 122) = 6.65, $p < .05$). When *all* events indicated by the participants were considered, the difference between the two groups (though in the same direction) did not approach a conventional level of significance. Categorization of short explanations for the events written by the participants revealed that for all the events mentioned, there were no differences between Forum participants and nominees.

Relational change index. On this measure, Forum participants tended to report a larger number of relationships becoming "closer" in the previous year and a half (mean = 4.57), compared to nominees (mean = 2.11) ($t = 2.26$, $p < .05$), although there was no difference in the number of people who became more distant.

Degree of involvement questionnaire. When asked to indicate an organized activity outside of work with which they had been involved in the last year and one-half, the Forum or a Forum-related activity was mentioned by 41 out of the

57 Forum participants who responded to this item.[4] Subjects were also asked to weigh the costs associated with the activity against the benefits derived from it. No significant differences were found in the cost-benefit estimation between Forum participants who referred to a Forum activity and Forum participants who referred to other activities. In addition, no differences were found between the cost-benefit ratios indicated by either of these groups and those generated by nominees. The impact of the activity for the subjects' lives and the number of family members and friends who took part in it also did not differ between the three groups. The latter two findings are inconsistent with reports in the literature, from methodologically weak studies, on the major impact LGATs allegedly have on peoples' lives.

For the *Expectancy For Success Measure* and the *Private Conceptions of Personal Change* questionnaire, there were no significant, systematic differences between Forum participants and nominees.

---

[4]It should be noted that for the degree of involvement questionnaire, the Forum and other representative activities (e.g., Elks, TM and Sierra Club) were mentioned to the subjects as examples of possible activities to consider when responding.

Chapter IV
Discussion

The present study is the first performed to evaluate the outcome of the Forum, an LGAT which has been in operation since January 1985 and which has attracted over 120,000 participants. It is also one of the first studies in the realm of LGAT evaluation to employ an appropriate control group, to correct for other difficulties associated with past LGAT research such as response set bias, and to employ a comprehensive outcome assessment battery. Overall, this study permits a more definitive conclusion than previous research regarding the effect of LGAT participation.

The outcome data can be examined to address the following questions: (a) to what extent, if any, is the Forum detrimental to participants' well-being? and (b) to what extent, if any, does Forum participation lead to positive changes? We will review the implications of the results for each of these questions, in turn.

Possible Negative Effects of Forum Participation

The present study is the first to assess potential negative changes in mental health from LGATs using an accepted index of clinical symptomatology. The data revealed no negative effects of Forum participation on any of the dimensions of symptomatology measured by the Brief Symptom Inventory. Negative effects of Forum participation could also have been revealed on any of the indices of well-being employed in the study (e.g., the findings could have indicated reduced self-esteem, or life satisfaction), but such results were not observed. Other potential indicators of negative outcomes were the participants' listing of negative events occurring in the year following the Forum (e.g., being fired from work or experiencing a significant failure), or finding negative changes in the participant's social network (e.g., losing network members or experiencing increased psychological distance from them). However, with the exception of one univariate effect, no evidence of negative effects was found on any of the measures, especially for the more reliable multivariate analyses. At least in the case of the Forum, which was the focus of the present research, the findings provide a counterpoint to the concern that has been expressed by clinicians and others that LGATs could have harmful psychological effects.

Possible Positive Outcomes of Forum Participation

Many of the potential favorable outcomes of the Forum were assessed on constructs represented in the multivariate analyses (i.e., Positive and Negative Affect, Health, Perceived Control, Social Functioning, Life Satisfaction, Self-Esteem, and Daily Coping). On seven of these eight dimensions, there were no significant short- or long-term multivariate treatment effects. On one, Perceived Control, the short- but not the long-term multivariate comparison with the nominees revealed that Forum participants became more internally oriented. Since Forum participants were also found to be more internal than nominees initially, it appears that the Forum attracts people who subscribe to "internal" beliefs (see Klar, 1990, for an extended discussion), and that these individuals may become even more internally oriented.

In contrast to the multivariate analyses, which indicated no long-term effect for Perceived Control, the univariate analyses revealed some indications of a long-term effect for two of the three indicators of this construct. However, since in the present context the multivariate analyses are more reliable for estimating treatment effects, the overall conclusion must be that no long-term effects were found on this dimension. Even if a significant long-term effect had been observed for perceived control, given that Forum participants were initially higher on this dimension, this alone could not be viewed as a dramatic shift in the participants' world views, but rather as an enhancement of a previously held system of beliefs.

In addition to the variables contained in the eight multivariate constructs, univariate techniques were used to examine more than 40 additional variables which could reflect possible favorable outcomes. The short- and long-term univariate analyses revealed only a few scattered differences between participants and nominees that could be considered consistent with some of the Forum emphases (e.g., better reported sleep quality). Taken in the context of the large number of variables assessed in the study and bearing in mind that none of these differences appeared in both the short- and long-term univariate analyses, these findings should not be considered to indicate robust effects.

Overall, although several minor, potentially positive effects were observed that could be associated with Forum participation, the general picture is one of stability rather than change, in the univariate as well as the more rigorous multivariate analyses. There was clearly no evidence of a dramatic shift on dimensions related to subjective well-being, perceived life satisfaction, or world view. In fact, with the exception of the short-term multivariate results for Perceived Control, there was no appreciable effect on any dimension which could reflect positive change.

Mediational Models of Positive Effects of Forum Participation

The analyses discussed thus far test the assumption that Forum participation, in and of itself, is necessary and sufficient to elicit benefits. However, it is possible that any benefits of the Forum are not direct, but occur in combination with other necessary factors (e.g., a change in "world view"; becoming part of an informal support group consisting of fellow Forum participants). It should be noted that such mediational models are based on the researchers' speculations — the Forum sponsors do not make such claims and instead, promise direct effects.

Since the design of the present study permitted the testing of mediational hypotheses, two that seemed plausible to the researchers were examined. The first assessed the possible mediating role of changes in world view (as reflected by changes in Perceived Control) in any beneficial effects of Forum participation. In effect, it assumed that the beneficial consequences of the Forum would be evidenced only for those who showed increased perceptions of control as a result of participation. According to this hypothesis, the Forum may lead to a shift in some participants' perceptions of internal control. The increased internality resulting from the Forum would then lead to other positive changes (e.g., more initiative, more coordinated action toward goals, more realistic goal setting), which would result in increased life satisfaction and well-being. Since much Forum content is directed toward increasing personal responsibility and perceived control (Shaw, 1977; Yalom, 1980), and since control has been related to well-being and psychological adjustment in the literature (Brannigan, Rosenberg, & Loprete, 1977; Kilmann, Laval, & Wanlass, 1978; Wolk & Kurtz, 1975), this model seemed reasonable.

Nevertheless, analyses of the paths represented in the model did not show an effect of increased internality on any of the outcome variables. One reason for this lack of effect could be the small number of subjects utilized in the analysis, since only those who completed all three sets of outcome measures could be included. To partially overcome this limitation, another model was created which ignored the pre-test measurement, and thus enabled the inclusion of subjects from Group 2. The analysis of this model also did not support the mediational role of perceived control.

A second plausible mediational hypothesis is that Forum participation is only an initial step in the change process. To produce beneficial effects, according to this model, participation must be supplemented by additional Forum activities (e.g., "graduate seminars") which in addition to their content, enhance the possibility of forming a social network supportive of Forum values, and of working toward personal goals. According to this hypothesis, the Forum serves primarily as an introduction for later "graduate" work in more concrete areas (e.g., seminars focusing on intimate and sexual relationships, creativity, excellence, leadership). These activities emphasize the importance of creating informal peer support groups and working toward attaining personal goals and allow participants an opportunity for coordinated action toward such goals. Although there are good reasons for assuming that involvement in subsequent Forum-related activities may mediate outcomes, they are not described by the Forum sponsors as a requisite for achieving results.

The hypothesis that involvement affects outcome can be tested by using an indication of involvement as a mediating variable. Our operationalization of involvement was to compute a measure of each individual's participation in post-Forum activities (i.e., graduate seminars, etc.), based on the actual hours required by these activities.[1] This index was included as a mediating variable in the model. As with the perceived control mediation hypothesis, in addition to the initial analysis, an additional one was performed including subjects from Group 2 to increase the statistical power. Neither revealed any effect of involvement on long-term outcome for any of the conceptual dimensions. Again, it should be kept in mind that the statistical power was significantly lower than for the direct effects models.

While the two analyses presented above do not exhaust the possibilities for mediational models of LGAT outcome that could be tested, they do represent the major ones suggested by the psychological literature and a consideration of Forum content. This should not discourage attempts to look for other possible mediators or moderators of potential outcome effects.

Alternative Explanations for the Results

Are the present results representative of true Forum outcome, or are there biasing factors that could have caused our overall findings of no appreciable treatment effects? We will discuss several such possibilities below.

1) *Selective participation and attrition.* Participation in the present study was voluntary: Individuals who took the Forum could decide whether or not they wanted to participate in the research. If research participants are not representative of the overall population that experiences an LGAT treatment, results may be biased. Analyses suggested that on demographic dimensions and on subsequent involvement in post-Forum activities, Forum participants who took part in the present research were comparable, overall, to those who participated in the Forum in the location and time period during which the study was completed. This lowers the likelihood that our findings are representative of only a specific subpopulation of Forum participants.

---

[1]This index was computed without identifying the subjects by name. In addition, it did not take volunteer hours into account. However, it is reasonable to assume that volunteer hours correlate with graduate seminar hours.

Another source of bias occurs if those who initially agree to take part in a study drop out selectively. When volunteer subjects are required to respond to questionnaires more than once with intervening periods of time, there are commonly problems with attrition. These become more serious when there are greater intervals between the initial testing and the follow-up testing. As more time elapses, more of the original subjects are unable to be contacted for participation, and more may simply lose interest in further participation. In the present research, comparisons between Forum participants who completed the pre- and post-measures and those who failed to return the post-test (but who were eligible to take part in the study) revealed only four significant differences out of a possible 138. Thus, selective attrition is unlikely to play an important role in accounting for the present findings.

Our findings that study participants appeared to be representative of Forum participants overall, and that attrition was not selective, may be due in part to the fact that in the current study, the LGAT evaluation was separated from the LGAT itself. In typical evaluation studies, participation and subsequent attrition may frequently be confounded with attitudes toward the program under evaluation (e.g., the more satisfied the person is with the program, the more inclined he or she will be to participate initially, or to continue to participate in the research). Program organizers may even have better records of participants who are satisfied and continue their involvement, making them easier to contact for follow-up research. The potential confound of attitudes toward the program with initial study participation and later attrition is reduced when data collection is separated from the program being evaluated.

2) *Insincere responses.* In any study, there is the possibility that subjects may not respond honestly. They could try to present themselves in a socially desirable way or might respond randomly to the questionnaire. There are several ways to estimate the likelihood of either of these possibilities. The former can be assessed by using a social desirability measure. In the present study, the univariate analysis of the Marlowe-Crowne Social Desirability Index (Crowne & Marlowe, 1960) did not reveal any systematic differences between groups, or between the measures. It is not the case that subjects in some conditions responded in a more socially desirable manner than others, or that certain measures elicited more socially desirable responses than others. Thus, the possibility that social desirability is responsible for the results obtained can be ruled out. The latter possibility, that subjects responded randomly to the lengthy questionnaire, can be addressed by considering the stability of the measures across the different testing intervals as an indicator of random responses. The high stability that was found in most variables across measurements argues against the possibility that the results could be explained by this factor.

3) *Ceiling effects.* Ceiling effects occur when subjects are already at the extreme on the dimensions being measured and there is no room for change. This

possibility can be ruled out almost entirely in the current context because the only dimension on which prospective participants were relatively close to the endpoint was Perceived Control. The pre-test mean for prospective Forum participants was 9.22 (out of 14) on the adapted version of Rotter's (1966) I-E scale, 50 (out of 66) on the Wallston et al. (1976) Health Locus of Control questionnaire and 7.33 (out of 10) on the Control over Hassles and Pleasant Events measure. While relatively high, these scores do not preclude the possibility of further change—in fact, such change was evidenced in the present research.

4) *Diffusion of effects.* Due to the nature of LGATs, it is possible that the benefits of participation may vary from one participant to another (e.g., one person may quit smoking; another may improve his or her relationship with a parent). If this were the case, it could be difficult to capture such individual outcomes as main effects of treatment, as was attempted in this study. This possibility was recognized at the design stage of the current research, and to guard against it, many global measures of well-being were included in the questionnaire. If an important "breakthrough" had occurred for a particular subject (e.g., if he or she had solved an important personal problem), this should have been reflected in one of these measures. Thus, it is unlikely that a "diffusion of effects" plays a major role in accounting for the present results.

5) *Contagion of the treatment to the control subjects.* Another possible alternative interpretation for the lack of treatment effects is that both Forum participants and nominee control subjects could have been influenced by the treatment. The participants were exposed to it directly, and the nominees could have been exposed to it through interaction with the participants. (For a complete discussion of contagion effects, see Cook & Campbell, 1979). The possibility of treatment contagion is especially relevant in the present context because LGAT participants are asked to "share" their experiences with members of their social network (Bry, 1976; Winstow, 1986). If there were "contagion," this could lead to a masking of the treatment effect (i.e., comparisons of Forum participants to nominees would yield no treatment effect, while in fact both groups had changed).

The possibility of contagion could be tested in two independent ways. First, if the nominees were indeed deriving significant personal benefits from indirect contact with the LGAT, it is likely that at least some of them would have sought to participate in the Forum during the year and one-half after their friends had taken it. Checking the nominees' follow-up questionnaires argues against this possibility; practically none of them reported taking the Forum in this period of time. Still another alternative is that the nominees would not take the LGAT, but rather enjoy it vicariously by being in close contact with those who participated in it. A test of this possibility reveals that nominees did not maintain close contact with Forum participants. Only a very small minority of the members in the nominees' social network were people who took the Forum. Thus, the possibility of contagion from Forum participants to nominees does not look very probable.

A final way to test the possibility of contagion is by looking at the absolute change in both groups from the pre-test to the follow-up. If there were contagion from Forum participants to nominees, *both* groups would have evidenced change from pre- to follow-up. Though the complications of using group means as indicators of treatment effects have been discussed earlier, they are nevertheless informative. A close look at the means of the various measures in Table 3.9 suggests that both groups remained remarkably stable, and fails to support the "contagion" interpretation, which would require major change from pre-test to follow-up in *both* groups.

6) *Representativeness of the outcome assessment.* A final possibility is that the outcome dimensions assessed did not coincide well with the domains in which the Forum was designed to have effects. If this were the case, the Forum could have had effects which were simply not captured by the outcome instrument. Clearly, the present research is the most comprehensive LGAT outcome study to date. It included a broad array of measures arrived at through a review of past research, observation of the Forum by the research team, and consultations with Forum executives. The measures consisted of well-validated instruments reflecting the "state of the art" in relevant psychological "state" and "trait" measures.

Nevertheless, the use of well-validated and tested instruments—though necessary to provide a reliable evaluation—also set limitations on the dimensions that could be assessed in the study. While some relevant domains within psychology (e.g., self-esteem, subjective well-being, negative life events, and social support) have been relatively well developed and have well-validated and tested measures with normative data, others have been relatively neglected. The latter domains (e.g., world view) have received much less attention, and as a result, were not as well represented in the study, although they may be significant for evaluating Forum outcome.

This points to several directions for future research. It is felt that future work should include more measures which tap world view. In the current research, the major indicator of world view was various measures of perceived control. Although it is related to a major Forum emphasis, perceived control measures should be supplemented by other indicators of world view, though few currently exist in the literature. There should also be refinements in the measures used to tap perceived control. Since individuals attracted to the Forum tend to report relatively high internal responses on such measures, more sensitive instruments are needed for precise evaluation. This may also be true in other domains where LGAT participants differ from the population at large. In addition, future LGAT research should include more objective measures of practical results (e.g., job promotions, increased productivity). It is noteworthy that the current research included no behavioral measures—it was limited to self-report questionnaires which subjects could complete in approximately an hour. How the current data would compare to behavioral data, interview data, or even a shorter questionnaire is unclear and should be addressed in future research.

Significance of the Results

Supporters of the Forum have claimed that participation causes epistemological shifts which should have measurable consequences. Given the "state of the art" in psychological measurement, the current study was able to tap some gross indicators of the assumed epistemological shifts and some broad indicators of their consequences (e.g., affective states, improved life satisfaction). Although there were no reliable long-term effects on dimensions related to epistemological shifts, the present findings contain some indications of short-term Forum outcome--there were changes in perceived control. However, it is noteworthy that on this dimension, Forum participants differed from nominee controls even before Forum participation. Overall, the picture is one of *stability* rather than psychological change. If the Forum had wide ranging psychological effects, we believe that they would have been evidenced in the current research.

References

Andrews, F. M., & Crandall, R. (1976). The validity of measures of self-reported well-being. *Social Indicators Research, 3*, 1-19.

Aronson, E., & Mills, J. (1959). The effects of severity of initiation on liking for a group. *Journal of Abnormal and Social Psychology, 59*, 177-181.

Aubrey, R. F. (1987). Ethical issues in psychotherapy research. *Counseling and Values, 31*, 139-140.

Back, K. W. (Ed.). (1978). *In search for community: Encounter groups and social change.* Boulder, CO: Westview Press.

Baer, D. M., & Stolz, S. B. (1978). A description of the Erhard Seminars Training (*est*) in the terms of behavioral analysis. *Behaviorism, 6*, 45-70.

Bartley, W. (1978). *Werner Erhard.* New York: Potter.

Beit-Hallahmi, B. (1987). The psychotherapy subculture: Practice and ideology. *Social Science Information, 26*, 475-492.

Berger, F. M. (1977). Awareness groups and psychiatry. *Bioscience Communication, 3*, 89-98.

Bergin, A. E. (1971). The evaluation of therapeutic outcomes. In A. E. Bergin & S. L. Garfield (Eds.), *Handbook of psychotherapy and behavior change* (2nd ed.) (pp. 217-270). New York: Wiley.

Brannigan, G. G., Rosenberg, L. A., & Loprete, L. J. (1977). Internal-external expectancy, maladjustment and psychotherapeutic intervention. *Journal of Personality Assessment, 41*, 71-78.

Brewer, M. (1975, August). We're gonna tear you down and put you back together. *Psychology Today*, pp. 35-40, 82, 88-89.

Bry, A. (1976). est: *60 hours that transform your life.* New York: Harper & Row.

Campbell, D. T., & Boruch, R. F. (1975). Making the case for randomized assignment to treatments by considering the alternatives: Six ways in which quasi-experimental evaluations tend to underestimate effects. In C. A. Bennett & A. A. Lumsdaine (Eds.), *Evaluation and experience: Some critical issues in assessing social programs* (pp. 195-246). New York: Academic Press.

Campbell, D. T., & Erlebacher, A. E. (1970). How regression artifacts in quasi-experimental evaluations can mistakenly make compensatory education look harmful. In J. Hellmuth (Ed.), *Compensatory education: A national debate: Vol. 3. Disadvantaged child.* New York: Brunner/Mazel.

Campbell, D. T., & Stanley, J. C. (1966). *Experimental and quasi-experimental designs for research.* Chicago: Rand McNally.

Cartwright, R. D., & Vogel, J. L. (1960). A comparison of changes in psychoneurotic patients during matched periods of therapy and no therapy. *Journal of Consulting Psychology, 24,* 121-127.

Cialdini, R. (1984). *Influence.* Glenview: Scott, Foresman.

Cinnamon, K., & Farson, D. (1979). *Cults and cons: The exploitation of the emotional growth consumer.* Chicago: Nelson-Hall.

Conway, F., & Siegelman, J. (1978). *Snapping.* Philadelphia: Lippincott.

Cook, T. D., & Campbell, D. T. (1979). *Quasi-experimentation: Design and analysis issues for field studies.* Chicago: Rand McNally.

Crowne, D. P., & Marlowe, D. (1960). A new scale of social desirability independent of psychopathology. *Journal of Consulting Psychology, 24,* 349-354.

Derogatis, L. R. (1975). *The Affects Balance Scale (ABS).* Baltimore: Clinical Psychometric Research.

Derogatis, L. R. (1977). *SCL-90 (Revised Version) Manual.* Baltimore: Clinical Psychometric Research.

Derogatis, L. R., Abeloff, M. D., & Melisaratos, N. (1979). Psychological coping mechanisms and survival time in metastic breast cancer. *Journal of the American Medical Association, 242,* 1504-1508.

Derogatis, L. R., & Melisaratos, N. (1983). The Brief Symptom Inventory: An introductory report. *Psychological Medicine, 13,* 595-605.

Diener, E., Larsen, R. J., Levine, S., & Emmons, R. A. (1985). Intensity and frequency: Dimensions underlying positive and negative affect. *Journal of Personality and Social Psychology, 48,* 1253-1265.

Efran, J. S., Lukens, M. D., & Lukens, R. J. (1986, March-April). It's all done with mirrors. *Networker,* pp. 41-49.

Emery, S. (1977). *Actualizations: You don't have to rehearse to be yourself.* Garden City, NY: Doubleday.

Erhard, W., & Gioscia, V. (1977). The *est* standard training. *Bioscience Communiçation, 3,* 104-122.

Erhard, W., & Gioscia, V. (1978). *est*: communication in context of compassion. *Current Psychiatric Therapy, 18,* 117-125.

est. (1977). *Herb Hamsher study of* est *mental health professionals.* San Francisco, CA: *est* Foundation.

est. (1980, September-October). The dialogue continues. San Francisco, CA: *est.* Foundation. *The Graduate Review,* pp. 3-11.

Feningstein, A., Scheier, M. F., & Buss, A. H. (1975). Public and private self-consciousness: Assessment and theory. *Journal of Consulting and Clinical Psychology, 43,* 522-527.

Fenwick, S. (1976). *Getting it: The psychology of* est. Philadelphia, PA: Lippincott.

Fibel, B., & Hale, W. D. (1978). The Generalized Expectancy for Success scale—A new measure. *Journal of Consulting and Clinical Psychology, 46,* 924-931.

Finkelstein, P., Wenegrat, B., & Yalom, I. (1982). Large group awareness training. *Annual Review of Psychology, 33,* 515-539.

Fisher, J. D., Silver, R. C., Chinsky, J. M., Goff, B., Klar, Y., & Zagieboylo, C. (1989). Psychological effects of participation in a large awareness training. *Journal of Consulting and Clinical Psychology, 57*(6), 747-755.

Fowler, F. J., Jr. (1984). *Survey research methods.* Beverly Hills, CA: Sage.

Frank, J. D. (1961). *Persuasion and healing.* Baltimore: Johns Hopkins University Press.

Frank, J. D. (1985). Further thoughts on the anti-demoralization hypothesis of psychotherapeutic effectiveness. *Integrative Psychiatry, 3,* 17-20.

Friedman, L. (1976). Defining psychotherapy. *Contemporary Psychoanalysis, 12,* 258-269.

Garfield, S. L. (1987). Ethical issues in research on psychotherapy. *Counseling and Values, 31,* 115-125.

Garfield, S. L., & Bergin, A. E. (1971). Therapeutic conditions and outcome. *Journal of Abnormal Psychology, 77,* 108-114.

Glass, L. L., Kirsch, M. A., & Parris, F. N. (1977). Psychiatric disturbances associated with Erhard Seminars Training: I. A report of cases. *American Journal of Psychiatry, 134,* 245-247.

Goldstein, A. P. (1960). Therapist and client expectation of personality change in psychotherapy. *Journal of Counseling Psychology, 7,* 180-184.

Gottlieb, B. M. (Ed.). (1988). *Marshaling social support: Formats, processes and effects.* Newbury Park, CA: Sage.

Greenwood, E. (Ed.). (1945). *Experimental sociology: A study in method.* New York: Octagon Books.

Grinker, R. R. (Ed.). (1956). *Toward a unified theory of human behavior.* New York: King's Crown Press.

Haaken, J., & Adams, R. (1983). Pathology as personal growth: A participant-observation study of Lifespring training. *Psychiatry, 46,* 270-280.

Hamsher, J. (1976). *The relationship between est and psychotherapy.* Unpublished manuscript available from Werner Erhard and Associates, 765 California Street, San Francisco, CA 94108.

Hartke, J. M. (1980). Ego development, cognitive style, and the *est* standard training. (Doctoral dissertation, Temple University). *Dissertation Abstracts International, 41* (6-B), 353.

Hazen, D. L. (1980). A follow-up of personality changes subsequent to the Erhard seminars training. (Doctoral dissertation, California School of Professional Psychology). *Dissertation Abstracts International, 41* (6-B), 2322.

Hirsch, B. J. (1979). Psychological dimensions of social networks: A multi-method analysis. *American Journal of Community Psychology, 7,* 263-272.

Hirsch, B. J. (1980). Natural support systems and coping with major life changes. *American Journal of Community Psychology, 8,* 159-172.

Hosford, R. E., Moss, C. S., Cavior, H., & Kernish, B. (1980). *Research on Erhard Seminars Training in a correctional institution.* Lompoc, CA: Federal Correctional Institution.

House, J. S., McMichael, A. J., Wells, J. A., Kaplan, B. H., & Landerman, L. R. (1979). Occupational stress and health among factory workers. *Journal of Health and Social Behavior, 20,* 139-160.

Joe, V. C. (1971). Review of the internal-external control construct as a personality variable. *Psychological Reports, 28,* 619-640.

Jöreskog, K. G., & Sörbom, D. (1986). *Analysis of linear structural relation-ships by maximum likelihood, instrumental variables, and least squares methods.* Mooresville, IN: Scientific Software.

Judd, C. M., & Kenny, D. A. (1981). *Estimating the effects of social interven-tions.* Cambridge, England: Cambridge University Press.

Kenny, D. A. (1975). A quasi-experimental approach to assessing treatment effects in the nonequivalent control group design. *Psychological Bulletin, 82,* 345-362.

Kenny, D. A. (1979). *Correlation and causality.* New York: Wiley.

Kidder, L. H., & Judd, C. M. (1986). *Research methods in social relations* (5th ed.). New York: Holt, Rinehart, & Winston.

Kilbourne, B., & Richardson, J. T. (1984). Psychotherapy and new religions in a pluralistic society. *American Psychologist, 39,* 237-251.

Kilmann, P. R., Laval, R., & Wanlass, R. L. (1978). Locus of control and perceived adjustment to life events. *Journal of Clinical Psychology, 34,* 512-513.

Kirsch, M. A., & Glass, L. L. (1977). Psychiatric disturbances associated with Erhard Seminars Training: 2. Additional cases and theoretical considerations. *American Journal of Psychiatry, 134,* 1254-1258.

Klar, Y., Mendola, R., Fisher, J. D., Silver, R. C., Chinsky, J. M., & Goff, B. (1990). Characteristics of participants in a large group awareness training. *Journal of Consulting and Clinical Psychology, 58*(1).

Klar, Y., & Nadler, A. (1988). [Beliefs about change: Towards the construc-tion of a measurement]. Unpublished raw data. Tel Aviv University.

Klein, M. (1983). How *est* works. *Transactional Analysis Journal, 13,* 178-180.

Koch, S. (1973, Autumn). The image of man in encounter groups. *American Scholar*, pp. 636-652.

Lazarus, P. J., & Weinstock, S. (1984). Use of socimetric peer nominations in classifying socially ignored versus socially rejected children. *School Psychology International, 5*, 139-146.

Lefkowitz, M. M., & Tesiny, E. P. (1985). Depression in children: Prevalence and correlates. *Journal of Consulting and Clinical Psychology, 53*, 647-656.

Lewis, L. (1976.) *Erhard Seminars Training: A longitudinal study*. Unpublished doctoral dissertation, California School of Professional Psychology, San Francisco, CA.

Lieberman, M. A. (1987). Effects of large group awareness training on participants' psychiatric status. *American Journal of Psychiatry, 144*, 460-464.

Lieberman, M. A., Yalom, I. D., & Miles, M. B. (1973). *Encounter groups: First facts*. New York: Basic Books.

Lifespring. (1985). *The Lifespring Basic Training is a context in which the ability to experience and express self is transformed so that life is alive, purposeful and complete*. San Rafael, CA: Author.

Lifespring. (1986). *Scientific inquiry: A report on independent studies of the Lifespring trainings*. San Rafael, CA: Author.

Lifespring. (1987, June). *Lifespring News*. San Rafael, CA: Author.

Lifespring. (1989). *Lifespring: A breakthrough in adult education*. San Rafael, CA: Author.

Ling, T. M., Zausmer, D. M., & Hope, M. (1952). Occupational rehabilitation of psychiatric cases: A follow-up of 115 cases. *American Journal of Psychiatry, 109*, 172-176.

Lord, F. M. (1960). Large-scale covariance analysis when the control variable is fallible. *Journal of the American Statistical Association, 55*, 307-321.

McCardel, J., & Murray, E. J. (1974). Non-specific factors in weekend encounter groups. *Journal of Consulting and Clinical Psychology, 42*, 337-345.

Murray, E. J., & Jacobson, L. I. (1971). The nature of learning in traditional and behavioral psychotherapy. In A. E. Bergin & S. L. Garfield (Eds.), *Handbook of psychotherapy and behavior change* (2nd ed.) (pp. 709-747). New York: Wiley.

Norbeck, J. S., Lindsey, A. M., & Carrieri, V. L. (1981). The development of an instrument to measure social support. *Nursing Research, 30*, 264-269.

Norbeck, J. S., Lindsey, A. M., & Carrieri, V. L. (1983). Further development of the Norbeck Social Support Questionnaire: Normative data and validity testing. *Nursing Research, 32*, 4-9.

Ornstein, R., Swencionis, C., Deikman, A., & Morris, R. (1975). *A self-report survey: Preliminary study of participants in Erhard seminars training.* San Francisco, CA: *est* Foundation.

Paterson, C. R., Dickson, A. L., Layne, C. C. (1984). California Psychological Inventory profiles of peer-nominated assertives, unassertives, and aggressives. *Journal of Clinical Psychology, 40,* 534-538.

Paul, N. L., & Paul, B. B. (1978). The use of *est* as adjunctive therapy to family-focused treatment. *Journal of Marriage and Family Counselling, 4,* 51-61.

Paulus, P. B. (1980). *Psychology of group influence.* Hillsdale, NJ: Erlbaum.

Powers, E., & Witmer, H. (1951). An experiment in the prevention of delinquency. In A. E. Bergin & S. L. Garfield (Eds.), *Handbook of psychotherapy and behavior change.* New York: Wiley.

Reichardt, C. S. (1979). The statistical analysis of data from nonequivalent group designs. In T. D. Cook & D. T. Campbell (Eds.), *Quasi-experimentation: Design and analysis issues for field settings* (pp. 147-205). Chicago: Rand McNally.

Rhinehart, L. (1976). *The book of* est. New York: Holt, Rinehart, & Winston.

Richardson, J. T., Stewart, M., & Simmonds, R. B. (1978). Researching a fundamentalist commune. In J. Needleman & G. Baker (Eds.), *Understanding the new religions* (pp. 235-251). New York: Seabury Press.

Robinson, J. P., & Shaver, P. R. (1973). *Measures of social psychological attitudes* (Rev. ed.). Ann Arbor, MI: Institute for Social Research.

Rogers, C. (1970). *Carl Rogers on encounter groups.* New York: Harper & Row.

Rome, H. P. (1977). Limits of the human mind. *Psychiatric Annals, 7*(11), 11-32.

Rosen, R. D. (1977). *Psychobabble: Fast talk and quick cure in the era of feeling.* New York: Atheneum.

Rosenberg, M. (1965). *Society and the adolescent self-image.* Princeton, NJ: Princeton University Press.

Rosenberg, M. (1969). The conditions and consequences of evaluation apprehension. In R. Rosenthal & R. Rosnow (Eds.), *Artifact in behavioral research* (pp. 279-349). New York: Academic Press.

Ross, M., & Conway, M. (1984). Remembering one's own past: The construction of personal histories. In R. Sorrentino & E. T. Higgins (Eds.), *Handbook of motivation and cognition* (pp. 122-144). New York: Guilford.

Rossi, P. H., Freeman, H. E., & Wright, S. R. (1979). *Evaluation.* Beverly Hills, CA: Sage.

Rotter, J. B. (1966). Generalized expectancies for internal versus external control of reinforcement. *Psychological Monographs, 80* (Whole No. 609).

Sarason, I. G., Johnson, J. H., & Siegel, J. M. (1978). Assessing the impact of life changes: Development of the Life Experiences Survey. *Journal of Consulting and Clinical Psychology, 46*, 932-946.

Selltiz, C., Jahoda, M., Deutsch, M., & Cook, S. (1959). *Research methods in social relations.* New York: Holt, Rinehart, & Winston.

Sharp, D. E. A. (1985). *Coping with the death of a spouse: Ruminations and the use of activity among bereaved women.* Unpublished master's thesis, University of Waterloo, Ontario.

Shaw, R. (1977). Large-scale awareness training groups—Their implications for the mental health professional. *Bioscience Communication, 3*, 85-88.

Shoemaker, O. S., Erickson, M. T., & Finch, A. J. (1986). Depression and anger in third- and fourth-grade boys: A multimethod assessment approach. *Journal of Clinical Child Psychology, 15*, 290-296.

Simon, J. (1978). Observations on 67 patients who took Erhard seminars training. *American Journal of Psychiatry, 135*, 686-691.

Simon, R. (1986, March-April). Of quarterbacks and coaches. *Networker*, pp. 30-34.

Solomon, R. L. (1949). An extension of control group design. *Psychological Bulletin, 46*, 137-150.

Spiegel, J. P. (1983). Cultural aspects of psychoanalysis and the alternative therapies. *Journal of The American Academy of Psychoanalysis, 11*, 331-352.

Subotnik, L. (1972). Spontaneous remission: Fact or artifact? *Psychological Bulletin, 77*, 32-48.

Sudman, S., & Bradburn, N. M. (1974). *Response effects in surveys: A review and synthesis.* Chicago, IL: Aldine.

Tedeschi, J. T., Schlenker, B. R., & Bonoma, T. V. (1971). Cognitive dissonance: Private ratiocination or public spectacle? *American Psychologist, 26*, 685-695.

Tipton, S. M. (1982). *Getting saved from the sixties.* Berkeley: University of California Press.

Tondow, D. M., Teague, R., Finney, J., & LeMaistre, G. (1973). *Abstract of the Behaviordyne report on psychological changes measured after taking the Erhard seminars training.* Palo Alto, CA: Behaviordyne.

Tziner, A., & Dolan, S. (1982). Evaluation of a traditional selection system in predicting the success of females in officer training. *Journal of Occupational Psychology, 55*, 269-275.

Wallston, B. S., Wallston, K. A., Kaplan, G. D., & Maides, S. A. (1976). Development and validation of the Health Locus of Control (HLC) scale. *Journal of Consulting and Clinical Psychology, 44*, 580-585.

Weiss, J. A. (1977). *Reported changes in personality, self-concept, and personal problems following Erhard seminars training.* Unpublished doctoral dissertation, California School of Professional Psychology, San Diego.

Werner Erhard & Associates. (1985). *The Forum (two weekends and one evening).* San Francisco: Author.

Werner Erhard & Associates. (1988). *The Forum.* San Francisco: Author.

Werner Erhard & Associates. (1989). *The Forum.* San Francisco: Author.

Winstow, F. (1986, March-April). Being there. *Networker*, pp. 20-29, 77-80.

Wolk, S., & Kurtz, J. (1975). Positive adjustment and involvement during aging and expectancy for internal control. *Journal of Consulting and Clinical Psychology, 43*, 173-178.

Wortman, C. B., & Silver, R. L. (1981). *SIDS loss: Psychosocial impact and predictors of coping* (Grant No. PHS MCJ260470) U.S. Public Health Service.

Wylie, R. C. (1974). *The self concept.* Lincoln, NB: University of Nebraska Press.

Yalom, I. D. (1980). *Existential psychotherapy.* New York: Basic Books.

Zander, A. F. (1985). *The purposes of groups and organizations.* San Francisco: Jossey-Bass.

Zilbergeld, B. (1983). *The shrinking of America.* Boston: Little, Brown.

Appendix A
The Study Measures

The Quality of Life in North America

1987-1988

University of Connecticut

University of Waterloo

Brief Symptom Inventory and Affects Balance Scale (items 1-40)[1]

In addition to having different feelings, people also may experience their feelings with varying degrees of intensity and for varying lengths of time. Please circle the intensity and time description that best fits your experience, on the average, for each emotion named in questions 41-48.

41 a. When you felt <u>happy</u> this past week, in general how happy did you feel?

0	1	2	3	4
Did Not Feel Happy (skip to 42)	Mildly Happy	Moderately Happy	Very Happy	Extremely Happy

   b. In general, how long did this feeling last?

1	2	3	4	5	6
Several Minutes Or Less	About An Hour	Several Hours	Most Of The Day	A Few Days	Almost The Entire Week

42 a. When you felt <u>satisfied</u> this past week, in general how satisfied did you feel?

0	1	2	3	4
Did Not Feel Satisfied (skip to 43)	Mildly Satisfied	Moderately Satisfied	Very Satisfied	Extremely Satisfied

   b. In general, how long did this feeling last?

1	2	3	4	5	6
Several Minutes Or Less	About An Hour	Several Hours	Most Of The Day	A Few Days	Almost The Entire Week

---

[1]The Brief Symptom Inventory and the Affects Balance Scale are copyrighted scales and are not reprinted here. They are obtainable from: Clinical Psychometric Research, Inc., P.O. Box 619, Riderwood, MD 21139.

43 a. When you felt <u>vigorous</u> this past week, in general how <u>vigorous</u> did you feel?

0	1	2	3	4
Did Not Feel Vigorous (skip to 44)	Mildly Vigorous	Moderately Vigorous	Very Vigorous	Extremely Vigorous

  b. In general, how long did this feeling last?

1	2	3	4	5	6
Several Minutes Or Less	About An Hour	Several Hours	Most Of The Day	A Few Days	Almost The Entire Week

44 a. When you felt <u>affectionate</u> this past week, in general how affectionate did you feel?

0	1	2	3	4
Did Not Feel Afféctionate (skip to 45)	Mildly Affectionate	Moderately Affectionate	Very Affectionate	Extremely Affectionate

  b. In general, how long did this feeling last?

1	2	3	4	5	6
Several Minutes Or Less	About An Hour	Several Hours	Most Of The Day	A Few Days	Almost The Entire Week

45a. When you felt <u>nervous</u> this past week, in general how nervous did you feel?

0	1	2	3	4
Did Not Feel Nervous (skip to 46)	Mildly Nervous	Moderately Nervous	Very Nervous	Extremely Nervous

  b. In general, how long did this feeling last?

1	2	3	4	5	6
Several Minutes Or Less	About An Hour	Several Hours	Most Of The Day	A Few Days	Almost The Entire Week

46 a. When you felt <u>miserable</u> this past week, in general how miserable did you feel?

0	1	2	3	4
Did Not	Mildly	Moderately	Very	Extremely
Feel Miserable	Miserable	Miserable	Miserable	Miserable
(skip to 47)				

    b. In general, how long did this feeling last?

1	2	3	4	5	6
Several	About	Several	Most Of	A Few	Almost The
Minutes	An Hour	Hours	The Day	Days	Entire Week
Or Less					

47 a. When you felt <u>guilty</u> this past week, in general how guilty did you feel?

0	1	2	3	4
Did Not	Mildly	Moderately	Very	Extremely
Feel Guilty	Guilty	Guilty	Guilty	Guilty
(skip to 48)				

    b. In general, how long did this feeling last?

1	2	3	4	5	6
Several	About	Several	Most Of	A Few	Almost The
Minutes	An Hour	Hours	The Day	Days	Entire Week
Or Less					

48 a. When you felt irritable this past week, in general how <u>irritable</u> did you feel?

0	1	2	3	4
Did Not	Mildly	Moderately	Very	Extremely
Feel Irritable	Irritable	Irritable	Irritable	Irritable

    b. In general, how long did this feeling last?

1	2	3	4	5	6
Several	About	Several	Most Of	A Few	Almost The
Minutes	An Hour	Hours	The Day	Days	Entire Week
Or Less					

We are interested in getting an idea of how you feel about various aspects of
your life. Using the scale below (0 - 7), please write the number, in the space to
the left of each item, that best corresponds to your feelings about each aspect of
your life.

> 0 = Delighted
> 1 = Pleased
> 2 = Mostly Satisfied
> 3 = Mixed (About equally satisfied and dissatisfied)
> 4 = Mostly Dissatisfied
> 5 = Unhappy
> 6 = Terrible
> 7 = Not Applicable; No feelings on this aspect of life, etc.

____ 1. My love relationship or marriage

____ 2. My children and being a parent

____ 3. My degree of recognition, success

____ 4. My financial situation

____ 5. My health

____ 6. My personal growth and development

____ 7. My exercise and physical recreation

____ 8. My religion, spiritual life

____ 9. My sex life

____ 10. The way my spouse or lover's life is going

____ 11. My friends and social life

____ 12. My physical attractiveness

____ 13. The degree to which I make a contribution to others

____ 14. Balance of time between my work, family, leisure, home
          responsibilities, etc.

____ 15. My life as a whole

Now we're going to ask you some questions about your health and health practices. We realize that some of the following questions are personal in nature. Please be assured that all information you give us is kept completely confidential. Fill in or circle the appropriate answer for each question.

1. Do you currently have any continuous or recurrent medical condition such as diabetes, cancer, high blood pressure, ulcers, heart conditions, etc.?

     Yes   No   (If no, skip to question #3)

2. If Yes, what is it? _____

3. In the <u>past week</u>, how much has your physical health limited your activity level at work (work in and out of the home, including housework)?

0	1	2	3	4
Not At All	Just A Little	Some	Quite A Bit	A Great Deal

4. In the <u>past week</u>, how much has your physical health kept you from doing things outside of work that you wanted to do?

0	1	2	3	4
Not At All	Just A Little	Some	Quite A Bit	A Great Deal

5. Compared to other persons your age, how is your health?

0	1	2	3
Poor	Fair	Good	Excellent

6. In the last month, how many times have you been to a doctor, clinic or hospital for something other than a regular check-up (a physical)?

        0 = No Visits
        1 = 1 - 2 Visits
        2 = 3 - 4 Visits
        3 = 5 - 6 Visits
        4 = 7 - 8 Visits
        5 = 9 or more visits

7. Was this an increase, decrease, or no change in the number of visits compared to the previous month?

0	1	2
Decrease	No Change	Increase

8. In the <u>past week</u>, how often were you satisfied with your night's sleep?

0	1	2	3	4
Never	Rarely	Some Of The Time	Most Of The Time	Always

9. In the <u>past week</u>, how often did you awaken feeling refreshed?

0	1	2	3	4
Never	Rarely	Some Of The Time	Most Of The Time	Always

10. In the <u>past week</u>, how often have you had restless or disturbed sleep?

0	1	2	3	4
Never	Rarely	Some Of The Time	Most Of The Time	Always

11. In the <u>past week</u>, how often have you felt the need to sleep more than usual?

0	1	2	3	4
Never	Rarely	Some Of The Time	Most Of The Time	Always

12. How often are you dieting to lose weight?

0	1	2	3	4
Never	Rarely	Some Of The Time	Most Of The Time	Always

13. How often do you engage in binge eating (i.e., eating large amounts of food rapidly)?

0	1	2	3	4
Almost Never	Rarely	Some Of The Time	Most Of The Time	Almost Always

14. In the past week, how often did you binge eat?

        Times per week _____

15. Do you smoke cigarettes, cigars or a pipe?

        Yes   No   (If no, skip to question 17)

    a. If cigarettes: During the past week how many did you smoke per day?

        Cigarettes _____

    b. If cigars or a pipe: During the past week how many cigars or pipe-fills of tobacco did you smoke per day?

        Cigars and/or pipe-fills _____

16. Are you currently trying to cut down or quit smoking?

        Yes   No

17. Do you drink alcoholic beverages?

        Yes   No   (If No, go to question 22)

18. During the past week, on how many days did you drink <u>any</u> alcoholic beverages? _____   (If 0, go to question 22)

19. When you did drink alcoholic beverages during the past week, how many drinks did you usually have per day? (A drink would consist of a one ounce shot, a glass of wine, or a beer.) _____

20. During the past week, what is the largest number of drinks you had at one time? _____

21. During the past week, have there been any problems between you and either your family or friends because you drank alcoholic beverages?

1	2	3	4
Never	Hardly Ever	Sometimes	Many Times

22. In the <u>past week</u>, have you taken any over-the-counter drugs such as diet pills, cough medicine, aspirin, etc.?

1	2	3	4
Never Taken	Rarely Taken	Sometimes Taken	Regularly Taken

23. In the <u>past week</u>, have you taken any street drugs such as PCP, Uppers, Downers, Speed, Quaaludes, Mescaline, Marijuana, Heroin, Cocaine, Methadone, etc.?

1	2	3	4
Never Taken	Rarely Taken	Sometimes Taken	Regularly Taken

24. In the past week, how often have you taken any medications <u>prescribed</u> for you by a physician such as tranquilizers, sleeping pills, valium, librium, or darvon?

1	2	3	4
Never Taken	Rarely Taken	Sometimes Taken	Regularly Taken

Below is a series of questions designed to determine the way in which different people view certain important health-related issues. Each item is a belief statement with which you may agree or disagree. Using the scale below, please write a number in the space to the left of each statement to indicate the extent to which you agree or disagree with it. The more strongly you agree with a statement, the higher the number you indicate will be; the more strongly you disagree with a statement, the lower the number will be.

1	2	3	4	5	6
Strongly Disagree	Moderately Disagree	Slightly Disagree	Slightly Agree	Moderately Agree	Strongly Agree

_____25. If I take care of myself, I can avoid illness.

_____26. Whenever I get sick it is because of something I've done or not done.

_____27. Good health is largely a matter of good fortune.

_____28. No matter what I do, if I am going to get sick I will get sick.

____29. Most people do not realize the extent to which their illnesses are controlled by accidental happenings.

____30. I can only do what my doctor tells me to do.

____31. There are so many strange diseases around that you can never know how or when you might pick one up.

____32. When I feel ill, I know it is because I have not been getting the proper exercise or eating right.

____33. People who never get sick are just plain lucky.

____34. People's ill health results from their own carelessness.

____35. I am directly responsible for my health.

We'd like to ask you a number of questions about how you feel about yourself. Express your agreement or disagreement with each item using the scale below (1 - 4). Place the appropriate number in the space to the left of each statement.

1	2	3	4
Strongly Disagree	Disagree	Agree	Strongly Agree

____ 1. I feel that I'm a person of worth, at least on an equal basis with others.

____ 2. I feel that I have a number of good qualities.

____ 3. All in all, I am inclined to feel that I am a failure.

____ 4. I am able to do things as well as most other people.

____ 5. I feel I do not have much to be proud of.

____ 6. I take a positive attitude toward myself.

____ 7. On the whole, I am satisfied with myself.

____ 8. I wish I could have more respect for myself.

____ 9. I certainly feel useless at times.

___ 10. At times, I think I am no good at all.

Work Activities[2]

This measure is to be filled out by someone who is employed by someone. If this not your <u>current</u> work situation, please call (203) 486-5917 so we can send you the appropriate measure. Now we would like to ask you some questions about your work. When answering the questions, we would like to find out how things have been during the past <u>month</u>. Please circle the appropriate number or fill in the answer where necessary.

1. Are you employed in a full or part-time job?

    1 Full-time   2 Part-time

2. What kind of work do you do?

    Title: _____   Type of Work: _____

3. How long have you been employed in your current job?

    Years: _____   Months: _____

Now we would like to ask you some specific questions about how you have been feeling in the past <u>month</u> about your work.

4. During the past <u>month,</u> how often have you been bothered by each of the following in your work?

    a) Feeling you have too much responsibility for the work of others?

0	1	2	3	4
Not At All	Rarely	Sometimes	Rather Often	Nearly All The Time

    b) Having to do or decide things where mistakes could be quite costly?

0	1	2	3	4
Not At All	Rarely	Sometimes	Rather Often	Nearly All The Time

    c) Not having enough help or resources to get the job done well?

0	1	2	3	4
Not At All	Rarely	Sometimes	Rather Often	Nearly All The Time

---

[2]Other versions of this measure were prepared for those who were self-employed, a student, or a homemaker.

d) Feeling that your work tends to interfere with your family life?

0	1	2	3	4
Not At All	Rarely	Sometimes	Rather Often	Nearly All The Time

e) Having to work overtime when you don't want to?

0	1	2	3	4
Not At All	Rarely	Sometimes	Rather Often	Nearly All The Time

f) Feeling trapped in a job you don't like but can't get out of?

0	1	2	3	4
Not At All	Rarely	Sometimes	Rather Often	Nearly All The Time

5. All in all, how satisfied would you say you are with your job?

0	1	2
Not At All Satisfied	Somewhat Satisfied	Very Satisfied

6. Knowing what you know now, if you had to decide all over again whether to take the same job you now have, what would you decide?

0   Decide definitely not to take the job
1   Have some second thoughts
2   Decide without hesitation to take the same job

7. In general, how well would you say your job measures up to the sort of job you wanted when you took it?

0   Not very much like what I wanted
1   Somewhat like what I wanted
2   Very much like what I wanted

8. If a good friend of yours told you he or she was interested in working in a job like yours for your employer, what would you tell him or her?

0   Advise him or her against it
1   Have doubts about recommending it
2   Strongly recommend it

9. In the next question we are interested in knowing how you see yourself in your work. Please circle the appropriate number on each of the following scales:

a) Successful	0	1	2	3	4	5	6	Not Successful
b) Important	0	1	2	3	4	5	6	Not Important
c) Doing My Best	0	1	2	3	4	5	6	Not Doing My Best

10. In this question we would like you to indicate how true you think each of the following statements is of your present job:

a) "I have an opportunity to develop my own special skills and abilities."

0	1	2	3
Not At All True	Not Too True	Somewhat True	Very True

b) "The work is interesting."

0	1	2	3
Not At All True	Not Too True	Somewhat True	Very True

c) "I am given a lot of freedom to decide how I do my work."

0	1	2	3
Not At All True	Not Too True	Somewhat True	Very True

d) "I am given a chance to do the things I like best."

0	1	2	3
Not At All True	Not Too True	Somewhat True	Very True

e) "I can learn new things."

0	1	2	3
Not At All True	Not Too True	Somewhat True	Very True

f) "I can use my skills, knowledge and abilities."

0	1	2	3
Not At All True	Not Too True	Somewhat True	Very True

g) "I can really believe in the value of what I am doing."

0	1	2	3
Not At All True	Not Too True	Somewhat True	Very True

h) "I can see the results of my own work."

0	1	2	3
Not At All True	Not Too True	Somewhat True	Very True

In these final work questions, we would like you to consider your reactions to the following situations and conditions at work. Please circle the number that most accurately reflects your attitude or behavior during the past month.

1. Working conditions at this job are fair for workers.

1	2	3	4	5
Definitely Agree	Somewhat Agree	Neither Agree Nor Disagree	Somewhat Disagree	Definitely Disagree

2. Suggestions about improvements in things related to my job are not considered by management.

1	2	3	4	5
Definitely Agree	Somewhat Agree	Neither Agree Nor Disagree	Somewhat Disagree	Definitely Disagree

3. I have ignored problems instead of bringing them to the attention of my supervisor.

0	1	2	3	4
Never	Seldom	Occasionally	Frequently	Always

4. Problems brought to the attention of management are dealt with justly.

1	2	3	4	5
Definitely Agree	Somewhat Agree	Neither Agree Nor Disagree	Somewhat Disagree	Definitely Disagree

5. Working conditions will remain the same regardless of whom I talk to or write to.

1	2	3	4	5
Definitely Agree	Somewhat Agree	Neither Agree Nor Disagree	Somewhat Disagree	Definitely Disagree

6. I have lied to avoid doing a task.

0	1	2	3	4
Never	Seldom	Occasionally	Frequently	Always

7. I cannot do anything to change company policies.

1	2	3	4	5
Definitely Agree	Somewhat Agree	Neither Agree Nor Disagree	Somewhat Disagree	Definitely Disagree

8. I am being fairly compensated for my job.

1	2	3	4	5
Definitely Agree	Somewhat Agree	Neither Agree Nor Disagree	Somewhat Disagree	Definitely Disagree

9. I have hidden broken things rather than reporting them.

0	1	2	3	4
Never	Seldom	Occasionally	Frequently	Always

A number of statements concerning personal attitudes and traits appear below. Please read each and decide whether the statement is true (T) or false (F) for you. Place a T or an F in the space to the left of each statement.

____ 1. No matter who I'm talking to, I'm always a good listener.

____ 2. I sometimes try to get even, rather than forgive and forget.

____ 3. I am quick to admit making a mistake.

____ 4. There have been times when I felt like rebelling against people in authority even though I knew they were right.

____ 5. I would never think of letting someone else be punished for my wrongdoing.

____ 6. At times I have wished that something bad would happen to someone I disliked.

____ 7. I am always attentive to the person I am with.

____ 8. I have sometimes taken unfair advantage of another person.

____ 9. I am always courteous even to people who are disagreeable.

____ 10. I sometimes feel resentful when I don't get my own way.

____ 11. I am always willing to admit when I make a mistake.

____ 12. There have been occasions when I took advantage of someone.

We are interested in getting some information about the type of events you have experienced in your life. The following list contains a number of events which sometimes have an impact on people's lives. In the last <u>five years</u>, if you have experienced any of these events, please put the month and year in which the event occurred in the first column opposite the event. Then, in the next column, please indicate the type of impact (if any) this event had on you <u>at</u> <u>the</u> <u>time</u> <u>it</u> <u>occurred</u>. Finally, we would like you to indicate the type of impact (if any) this event has on you <u>now</u>.

If you have experienced an event more than once in the last six years, name the event and give the dates and impact ratings on the lines at the end of section one. If you have experienced any event not listed here that had an important impact on you, please identify it and rate its impact using the blank lines at the end of section one.

−3	−2	−1	0	+1	+2	+3
Extremely Negative	Moderately Negative	Somewhat Negative	No Impact	Somewhat Positive	Moderately Positive	Extremely Positive

<u>Section One</u>   (Please use "+" and "-" signs)

EVENT	MO/YR	IMPACT THEN	IMPACT NOW
1. Marriage	_____	_____	_____
2. Detention in jail or comparable institution	_____	_____	_____
3. Death of close family member:			
a. spouse	_____	_____	_____
b. child	_____	_____	_____
c. mother	_____	_____	_____
d. father	_____	_____	_____
e. brother	_____	_____	_____
f. sister	_____	_____	_____
g. grandmother	_____	_____	_____
h. grandfather	_____	_____	_____
i. other (specify) _____	_____	_____	_____
4. Death of close friend	_____	_____	_____

−3	−2	−1	0	+1	+2	+3
Extremely Negative	Moderately Negative	Somewhat Negative	No Impact	Somewhat Positive	Moderately Positive	Extremely Positive

Section One   (Please use "+" and "-" signs)

EVENT	MO/YR	IMPACT THEN	IMPACT NOW
5. Major change in sleeping habits:			
a. much more sleep	____	____	____
b. much less sleep	____	____	____
6. Major change in eating habits			
a. much more food intake	____	____	____
b. much less food intake	____	____	____
7. Foreclosure on mortgage or loan	____	____	____
8. Outstanding personal achievement	____	____	____
9. Trouble with the police or the law :			
a. Minor law violation	____	____	____
b. Major law violation	____	____	____
10. Male: Wife/girlfriend's pregnancy	____	____	____
11. Female: Pregnancy	____	____	____
12. Changed work situation (different work responsibility, major change in working conditions, hours, etc.)	____	____	____
13. New job	____	____	____
14. Serious illness or injury of close family member:			
a. spouse	____	____	____
b. child	____	____	____
c. father	____	____	____
d. mother	____	____	____
e. sister	____	____	____
f. brother	____	____	____
g. grandfather	____	____	____
h. grandmother	____	____	____
i. other (specify) _____	____	____	____

-3	-2	-1	0	$+1$	$+2$	$+3$
Extremely	Moderately	Somewhat	No	Somewhat	Moderately	Extremely
Negative	Negative	Negative	Impact	Positive	Positive	Positive

Section One   (Please use "+" and "-" signs)

EVENT	MO/YR	IMPACT THEN	IMPACT NOW
15. Serious injury or illness of close friend...	_____	_____	_____
16. Sexual difficulties	_____	_____	_____
17. Trouble with employer (in danger of losing job, being suspended, demoted, etc.)	_____	_____	_____
18. Trouble with in-laws	_____	_____	_____
19. Major change in financial status			
a. a lot better off	_____	_____	_____
b. a lot worse off.................................	_____	_____	_____
20. Major change in closeness of family members			
a. increased closeness	_____	_____	_____
b. decreased closeness	_____	_____	_____
21. Gaining a new family member (through birth, adoption, family member moving in, etc.)	_____	_____	_____
22. Change in residence	_____	_____	_____
23. Marital separation from mate (due to conflict)..	_____	_____	_____
24. Major change in church activities			
a. increased attendance	_____	_____	_____
b. decreased attendance	_____	_____	_____
25. Marital reconciliation with mate...........	_____	_____	_____
26. Major change in number of arguments with spouse			
a. a lot more arguments	_____	_____	_____
b. a lot less arguments _____	_____	_____	_____
27. Married male: Change in wife's work outside the home (beginning work, ceasing work, changing to a new job, etc.)	_____	_____	_____

−3	−2	−1	0	+1	+2	+3
Extremely Negative	Moderately Negative	Somewhat Negative	No Impact	Somewhat Positive	Moderately Positive	Extremely Positive

Section One

(Please use "+" and "-" signs)

EVENT	MO/YR	IMPACT THEN	IMPACT NOW
28. Married female: Change in husband's work (loss of job, beginning new job, retirement, etc.)	_____	_____	_____
29. Major change in usual type and/or amount of recreation	_____	_____	_____
30. Borrowing more than $10,000 (buying home, business, etc.)	_____	_____	_____
31. Borrowing less than $10,000 (buying care, TV, getting school loan, etc)	_____	_____	_____
32. Being fired from job	_____	_____	_____
33. Male: Wife/girlfriend having abortion.	_____	_____	_____
34. Female: Having an abortion.	_____	_____	_____
35. Major personal illness or injury.	_____	_____	_____
36. Major change in social activities, e.g., parties, movies, visiting			
a. increased participation.	_____	_____	_____
b. decreased participation.	_____	_____	_____
37. Major change in living conditions of family (building new home, remodeling, deterioration of home, neighborhood, etc.)	_____	_____	_____
38. Divorce	_____	_____	_____
39. Retirement from work.	_____	_____	_____
40. Son or daughter leaving home (due to marriage, college, etc.)	_____	_____	_____
41. Separation from spouse (due to work, travel, etc.)	_____	_____	_____
42. Engagement.	_____	_____	_____
43. Break up of romantic relationship	_____	_____	_____

-3	-2	-1	0	$+1$	$+2$	$+3$
Extremely	Moderately	Somewhat	No	Somewhat	Moderately	Extremely
Negative	Negative	Negative	Impact	Positive	Positive	Positive

Section One   (Please use "+" and "-" signs)

EVENT	MO/YR	IMPACT THEN	IMPACT NOW
44. Leaving home for first time .... _____		_____	_____
45. Reconciliation with romantic partner ... _____		_____	_____
46. Being robbed or burglarized .... _____		_____	_____
47. Being sexually assaulted or abused .... _____		_____	_____
48. Being physically assaulted or abused .... _____		_____	_____
49. _____ .... _____		_____	_____
50. _____ .... _____		_____	_____
51. _____ .... _____		_____	_____
52. _____ .... _____		_____	_____
53. _____ .... _____		_____	_____

(Please fill out section two only if you are presently a student, otherwise skip to Section three.)

Section two: Student Only

54. Academic probation .... _____		_____	_____
55. Being dismissed from dormitory or other residence .... _____		_____	_____
56. Failing an important exam .... _____		_____	_____
57. Changing a major .... _____		_____	_____
58. Failing a course .... _____		_____	_____
59. Financial problems concerning school (in danger of not having sufficient money to continue) .... _____		_____	_____

If there are any stressful events that occurred more than 5 years ago that you still feel affect your life, please list each below and rate the impact as you have done above.

-3	-2	-1	0	$+1$	$+2$	$+3$
Extremely	Moderately	Somewhat	No	Somewhat	Moderately	Extremely
Negative	Negative	Negative	Impact	Positive	Positive	Positive

Section Three   (Please use "+" and "-" signs)

		IMPACT	IMPACT
EVENT	MO/YR	THEN	NOW

60. _____ ...._____   _____   _____
61. _____ ...._____   _____   _____
62. _____ ...._____   _____   _____
63. _____ ...._____   _____   _____
64. _____ ...._____   _____   _____

In addition to major problems, most of us are faced with many minor problems or hassles. For example, having something get lost, broken, or stolen; having an unexpected bill or being overcharged for something; being kept waiting in line for service, having too much to do, etc.

1. In the past week, how often would you say that hassles similar to these have occurred?

1	2	3	4	5
Almost	Not Too	Sometimes	Pretty	Almost
Never	Often		Often	Always

2. During the past week, when these hassles have occurred, how much did they bother or upset you?

1	2	3	4	5
Not At	Just A	Somewhat	Quite A	A Great
All	Little		Bit	Deal

3. During the past week, when these hassles occurred, how well do you feel you handled them?

1	2	3	4	5
Very	Pretty	Somewhat	Pretty	Very
Poorly	Poorly	Poorly	Well	Well

4. At this point in your life, how much control do you feel you have over whether or not <u>bad</u> things happen to you?

1	2	3	4	5
None	Just A Little	Some	Quite A Bit	A Great Deal

In addition to problems and hassles, people report pleasant events—for example, a good friend comes to visit, having an especially nice meal, doing something you really enjoy, etc.

5. In the <u>past week</u>, how often would you say that pleasant events similar to these have occurred?

1	2	3	4	5
Almost Never	Not Too Often	Sometimes	Pretty Often	Almost Always

6. During the <u>past week</u>, when pleasant events like these have occurred, how much happiness or pleasure have you received from them?

1	2	3	4	5
None At All	Just A Little	Some	Quite A Bit	A Great Deal

7. At this point in your life, how much control do you feel you have over whether or not <u>good</u> things happen to you?

1	2	3	4	5
None At All	Just A Little	Some	Quite A Bit	A Great Deal

This section of the questionnaire is designed to find out the way in which certain important events in our society affect different people. Each item consists of a pair of alternatives marked 0 or 1. Please select the one statement of each pair (and only one) which you more strongly believe to be the case as far as you are concerned. Be sure to select the one you actually believe to be more true rather than the one you think you should choose or the one you would like to be true. This is a measure of personal beliefs and there are no right or wrong answers.

Please answer these items carefully but do not spend too much time on any one item. Be sure to find an answer for every choice.

In some instances you may discover that you believe both statements or neither one. In such cases, be sure to select the one statement you more strongly believe to be the case as far as you are concerned. Also, try to respond to each item independently when making your choice: do not be influenced by your previous choices. Circle the "0" or "1" to the left of the statement you choose.

1. 0 In the long run people get the respect they deserve in this world.
    1 Unfortunately, an individual's worth often passes unrecognized no matter how hard he/she tries.

2. 0 Without the right breaks one cannot be an effective leader.
    1 Capable people who fail to become leaders have not taken advantage of their opportunities.

3. 0 In the case of the well prepared student there is rarely if ever such a thing as an unfair test.
    1 Many times exam questions tend to be so unrelated to course work that studying is really useless.

4. 0 Becoming a success is a matter of hard work; luck has little or nothing to do with it.
    1 Getting a good job depends mainly on being in the right place at the right time.

5. 0 The average citizen can have an influence in government decisions.
    1 This world is run by the few people in power, and there is not much the little guy can do about it.

6. 0 In my case getting what I want has little or nothing to do with luck.
    1 Many times we might just as well decide what to do by flipping a coin.

7. 0 Who gets to be the boss often depends on who was lucky enough to be in the right place first.
    1 Getting people to do the right thing depends upon ability; luck has little or nothing to do with it.

8. 0 As far as world affairs are concerned, most of us are the victims of forces we can neither understand, nor control.
    1 By taking an active part in political and social affairs the people can control world events.

9. 0 It is hard to know whether or not a person really likes you.
    1 How many friends you have depends on how nice a person you are.

10. 0 With enough effort we can wipe out political corruption.
    1 It is difficult for people to have much control over the things politicians do in office.

11. 0 Sometimes I can't understand how teachers arrive at the grades they give.
    1 There is a direct connection between how hard I study and the grades I get.

12. 0 Many times I feel that I have little influence over the things that happen to me.
    1 It is impossible for me to believe that chance or luck plays an important role in my life.

13. 0 People are lonely because they don't try to be friendly.
    1 There's not much use in trying too hard to please people, if they like you, they like you.

14. 0 What happens to me is my own doing.
    1 Sometimes I feel that I don't have enough control over the direction my life is taking.

Social Network List

The following questionnaire is designed to provide us with some information regarding the important people in your life. Please list each significant person in your life using the first two columns which appear to the right. Consider people who are important to you as well as those who provide personal support such as talking over problems or giving material aid.

Use only initials, and then indicate the relationship, as in the following example:

Example:

Initials	Relationship
1. D.L.	father
2. T.F.	mother
3. J.B.	friend
4. M.L.	minister

The following list may help you think of the people who are important to you.

- spouse or partner
- family members or relatives
- friends
- work or school associates
- neighbors
- health care providers
- counselor or therapist
- minister/priest/rabbi
- other

You do not have to use all of the 24 spaces. Since people vary in the number of people they consider important in their lives; use only as many spaces as you need.

Social Network List

Initials	Relationship	Activity
1. _____	_____	_____
2. _____	_____	_____
3. _____	_____	_____
4. _____	_____	_____
5. _____	_____	_____
6. _____	_____	_____
7. _____	_____	_____
8. _____	_____	_____
9. _____	_____	_____
10. _____	_____	_____
11. _____	_____	_____
12. _____	_____	_____
13. _____	_____	_____
14. _____	_____	_____
15. _____	_____	_____
16. _____	_____	_____
17. _____	_____	_____
18. _____	_____	_____
19. _____	_____	_____
20. _____	_____	_____
21. _____	_____	_____
22. _____	_____	_____
23. _____	_____	_____
24. _____	_____	_____

Note: For each of the following 10 questions the list above was repeated.

For each person you listed, please answer the following 8 questions by writing in the number that applies.

> 1 = Not at all
> 2 = A Little
> 3 = Moderately
> 4 = Quite a bit
> 5 = A great deal

Question 1. How much do you feel liked or loved in the presence of this person?

Question 2. How much do you feel respected or admired in the presence of this person?

Question 3. How much can you confide in this person?

Question 4. How much does this person agree with or support your actions or thoughts?

Question 5. If you need to borrow $10, obtain a ride to the doctor, or some other immediate help, how would this person usually help?

Question 6. How much do you like or love this person?

Question 7: How much do you respect or admire this person?

Question 8: Overall, how satisfied are you with your relationship with this person?

Question 9: How long have you known this person?

> 1 = less than 6 mos
> 2 = 6 to 12 mos
> 3 = 1 to 2 years
> 4 = 2 to 5 years
> 5 = more than 5 yrs

Question 10: How frequently do you usually have contact with this person (by phone, visit or letters)?

> 1 = daily
> 2 = weekly
> 3 = monthly
> 4 = a few times a yr
> 5 = once a yr or less

PLEASE BE SURE YOU HAVE RATED EACH PERSON ON EVERY QUESTION.

Please look at the Social Network list you just completed. Place the initials of the first 15 people from that list across the top of this chart, below the corresponding number. Then list the same people's initials next to the numbers down the left side of the chart. Put an X in the box at the intersection of any two people who have contact with each other personally, by phone, or by letter once a week or more.

EXAMPLE:

In this example, "D.L.", the father from the Social Network List sees the mother, "T.F.", once a week or more but neither see "J.B." once a week or more.

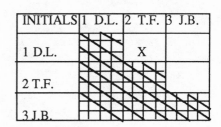

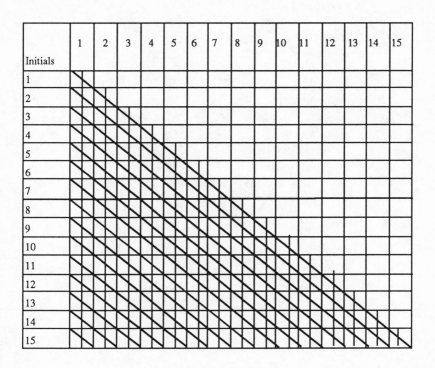

11. Given our interest in the quality of life, we would like to know the degree to which people important to you have participated in any self-awareness or self-improvement activities. If any of the people you have listed have, to your knowledge, participated in any such activities (e.g., TM, est, the Forum, Lifespring, etc.), please name the activity next to the person on the previous page in the column labelled "Activity".

12. During the past year, have you lost any important relationships due to moving, a job change, divorce or separation, death, or some other reason? (Please circle one.)

No   Yes

If Yes:

13a. Please indicate the number of persons from each category who are no longer available to you.

_____ spouse or partner
_____ family members or relatives
_____ friends
_____ work or school associates
_____ neighbors
_____ health care providers
_____ counselor or therapist
_____ minister/priest/rabbi
_____ other (specify) _____

13b. Overall, how much of your support was provided by these people who are no longer available to you? (Please circle one.)

0 = none at all
1 = a little
2 = a moderate amount
3 = quite a bit
4 = a great deal

Now we would like to find out how accurately the following statements describe your attitudes toward self-help, self-improvement, and self-awareness issues. Using the scale below, please write the number that best reflects how each statement describes you. Place the number in the space provided to the left of each statement.

> 1 = Very Unlike Me
> 2 = Somewhat Unlike Me
> 3 = Somewhat Like Me
> 4 = Very Much Like Me

_____ 1. I am the type who usually takes care of problems by myself.

_____ 2. I usually share personal problems only with close friends and family.

_____ 3. I am likely to recommend self-awareness activities to other people.

_____ 4. I know there must be something more to life that I have experienced so far.

_____ 5. I don't like to share my personal problems with anyone.

_____ 6. I think being involved in self-awareness activities is worthwhile.

_____ 7. The only reason I would do a self-awareness activity would be if I were pressured into it.

_____ 8. I feel there is a deeper meaning in life to be found.

_____ 9. In order to progress either personally or professionally, I feel self-awareness activities can be useful.

_____10. When I have problems, I think self-awareness activities can help me.

Given our interest in the quality of life, we would also like to ask you about your involvement in self-help, self-improvement, and/or self-awareness activities.

11. How often have you read self-help, self-improvement, and/or self-awareness books?

0	1	2	3
Never	Rarely	Sometimes	Frequently

12. Have you ever been involved in self-help, self-improvement, and/or self-awareness activities (including therapy or counseling)?

No   Yes

If YES, please list and give beginning and ending dates:

ACTIVITY	FROM	TO
a._____	a._____	_____
b._____	b._____	_____
c._____	c._____	_____
d._____	d._____	_____
e._____	e._____	_____
f._____	f._____	_____

We've created a series of items to give us general information about the people who are completing these questionnaires.

1. Do you live alone?

      Yes (skip to #3)   No

2. We would like to have some informatoin on who lives with you now. We don't need their name, just their age, their sex, and their relationship to you.

Members of the Household (identified by relationship to you)	Sex	Age
1.		
2.		
3.		
4.		
5.		
6.		
7.		
8.		

3. Do you have any other children who do not live with you? Please indicate the number and age(s) below.

                         #   Ages

(If none write "0")   _____   _____

4. What is your current religious preference?

       0   Protestant
       1   Jewish
       2   Catholic
       3   Other
       4   None

5. How important is religion in your life?

1	2	3	4	5
Not at All Important	Slightly Important	Somewhat Important	Moderately Important	Extremely Important

6. How often do you attend religious services?

1	2	3	4	5
Never	Rarely	Once Or Twice A Month	Once A Week	More Than Once a Week

7. Your race:

       0   White
       1   Black
       2   Hispanic
       3   Asian
       4   Native American
       5   Other

8. Do you consider yourself to be <u>primary</u>

       1   HETEROSEXUAL (physically attracted to a person or persons of the opposite sex)
       2   HOMOSEXUAL (physically attracted to a person or persons of the same sex)
       3   BISEXUAL (physically attracted to persons of either sex)

9. Who is the principal wage earner?
(e.g., husband, mother, father, self) _____

10. Please describe the usual occupation of the principal wage earner in your household. (If retired, describe the usual occupation before retirement.)

TITLE: _____

KIND OF WORK: _____

11. If not indicated in question 9, what is your usual occupation?

TITLE: _____

KIND OF WORK: _____

4. What was your annual income, before taxes, this past year?

    0   Under $8,000
    1     $ 8,000 to $12,000
    2     $12,000 to $20,000
    3     $20,000 to $30,000
    4     $30,000 to $50,000
    5     $50,000 to $75,000
    6   More than $75,000

5. What was the total annual income for your family (for yourself and family living with you) from all sources, before taxes, this past year?

    0   Under $8,000
    1     $ 8,000 to $12,000
    2     $12,000 to $20,000
    3     $20,000 to $30,000
    4     $30,000 to $50,000
    5     $50,000 to $75,000
    6   More than $75,000

14. What was the last grade or class you completed in school?
(Circle last year completed.)

School Grade   College/Vocational School

6th   7th   8th   9th   10th 11th 12th   1st   2nd   3rd   4th   5th

15. What is the hightest degree you have earned (B.A., M.D., M.B.A., etc.)?

_____

MEASURES USED ONLY IN THE FOLLOW UP

We would also like to know about any major events in the past year which had special significance for you (e.g., personal achievements, disappointments, meaningful experiences). Describe briefly up to three major events of the last year and using the list below, indicate the primary reason you believe it occurred by writing the number in the space provided. Please give the date of the event in the next space. After each event, reason, and date, please give a brief description of why the event was significant for you.

Reason for occurrence

1   I used/failed to use abilities I've had or acquired informally
2   I used/failed to use knowledge/understanding acquired through organized training/education
3   Occurred because of others
4   Occurred through the joint efforts of myself and others
5   Occurred through good luck
6   Occurred through God's will

1. Event _____ Reason _____ Date _____

Explanation_____

2. Event _____ Reason _____ Date _____

Explanation_____

3. Event _____ Reason _____ Date _____

Explanation_____

We would like to know a little more about the important people in your life.

1. In the past year and a half, with how many friends or family members have you experienced a major relationship change (e.g., in intimacy, in frequency of contact)? Many find it helpful to jot down a list of those with whom they were close a year and a half ago to help with this task. After reviewing those relationships of a year and a half ago and your current significant relationships, in the

spaces below, indicate the number of significant relationships which have become closer and the number which have become more distant in the past year and a half (if none, put a zero). Do not consider changes due to death or relocation.

# of Relationships which are closer _____

# of Relationships which are more distant _____

Now please list below the initials of three of these friends or family members with whom you feel the <u>most</u> change resulting in greater <u>closeness</u> has occurred (if there are fewer than three list as many as apply). After each person's initials, indicate their relationship to you (spouse, friend, mother, father, brother, sister, other relative, etc.). Then, using the list of reasons given below, indicate the <u>primary</u> and <u>secondary</u> reasons for the change by writing the number of <u>one</u> of the reasons from the list in each of the spaces provided. Finally, if you feel the reasons you have chosen from the list need explanation, please do so in the space provided.

<u>Reasons for Increased Closeness Statements</u>:

1   We discovered new shared interests
2   He/She was someone I could respect
3   The relationship was becoming more satisfying
4   We had developed greater trust between us
5   I was seeing greater similarity in attitudes and values
6   We had developed greater caring
7   I was liking the way I felt around this person
8   He/She was changing in positive ways
9   I was becoming a more accepting person
10   He/She was very generous
11   He/She made me feel good about myself
12   I began to care more

<u>People who became closer</u>

		Primary	Secondary
a. Initials_____ Relationship_____		Reason____	Reason____

Explanation _____

b. Initials_____ Relationship_____ Primary Reason____ Secondary Reason____

Explanation _____

c. Initials_____ Relationship_____ Primary Reason____ Secondary Reason____

Explanation _____

Please follow the same procedure for the three friends or family members with whom you feel the most change resulting in greater distance occurred. Remember to fill in both a primary and a secondary reason from the list below, after indicating their initials and relationship to you.

Reasons for Increased Distance Statements:

1   He/She changed in ways I could not accept
2   My feelings changed about the person
3   He/She was insensitive to me
4   We no longer shared the same interests
5   I had less available time
6   I had changed in ways he/she could not accept
7   His/her feelings changed
8   The relationship was holding us back
9   He/She betrayed a trust/agreement
10   He/She took more than he/she gave
11   The relationship had lost its meaning
12   There was no longer a sense of trust between us
13   He/she had less time for the friendship
14   We wanted different things from the friendship
15   My needs were not being met

People who became more distant

a. Initials_____ Relationship_____ Primary Reason____ Secondary Reason____

Explanation _____

b. Initials_____ Relationship_____ Reason____   Reason____

Explanation _____

| | | Primary | Secondary |
c. Initials_____ Relationship_____ Reason____   Reason____

Explanation _____

Degree of Involvement

We would like to know about some of your activities outside of work. In particular, we are interested in your involvement in organized activities and how it has contributed to the quality of your life, in the last year and a half.

List below the organized activity (e.g., Elks, Transcendental Meditation, Sierra Club) in which you most frequently took part, in the past year and a half. Be sure this is an organized group activity rather than an individual activity such as reading or tennis. Because of our focus on changes in the quality of life, if you have been involved in Transcendental Meditation, Lifespring, the Forum, est, or another growth oriented activity in the past year and a half please make it the activity on which you report, even if it has not been the most frequently attended.

Name of Activity: _____

Many people find there are costs, benefits, or some combination of the two associated with involvement in an organized activity. The following three questions deal with the relative impact of some typical costs and benefits associated with a variety of organized activities. Please answer the questions only for the one activity which you have indicated above.

1. Using the scale below, please rate the impact of each of the costs which follow by writing the appropriate number in the space to the left of each cost statement. Add any significant costs not listed in the spaces marked "other" and rate their importance.

<u>Scale</u>:

> 0 = No Impact
> 1 = A Slight Impact
> 2 = Some Impact
> 3 = Moderate Impact
> 4 = Strong Impact

<u>Cost Statements</u>

My association with the organization:

____ a. Took time away from friends and family
____ b. Created an added financial burden
____ c. Caused disapproval from friends/family for my involvement
____ d. Caused me to recognize that I could be doing things rather than making excuses for not doing them
____ e. Caused me to notice flaws in myself
____ f. Gave me burdensome responsibilities
____ g. (other) _____
____ h. (other) _____

2. Please assess the impact of the following benefits as you did with the costs. Remember to add and rate the importance of any benefits which are not listed in the spaces marked "other".

<u>Scale</u>:

> 0 = No Impact
> 1 = A Slight Impact
> 2 = Some Impact
> 3 = Moderate Impact
> 4 = Strong Impact

<u>Benefit Statements</u>

My association with the organization:

____ a. Gave me the opportunity to meet others socially
____ b. Gave me the opportunity for business and professional contacts
____ c. Exposed me to new ideas

____ d. Gave me a sense of belonging
____ e. Gave me insight into previously undeveloped parts of myself
____ f. Gave me the opportunity to develop new skills and aspects of myself
____ g. (other) _____
____ h. (other) _____

3. Considering the costs and benefits related to this activity, mark an "X" on the line below to indicate the degree to which the costs outweigh benefits or the benefits outweigh the costs. For example, an "X" in the far left space would indicate costs completely outweigh benefits. An "X" in the middle would indicate an even balance of costs and benefits.

Costs :____:____:____:____:____:____:____:____: Benefits

4. How often have you attended meetings or taken part in activities related to this group in the last year?

1	2	3	4
Frequently	Fairly Often	Occasionally	Rarely

# of meetings in last year:_____

Average # of hours per meeting:_____

5. Please describe the specific nature of your involvement (types of activities, offices or positions held, etc.).

_____

6. Briefly describe any future plans for involvement with this group.

_____

7. How important is the impact of this activity on the rest of your life?

1	2	3	4	5
Not at All Important	Slightly Important	Somewhat Important	Moderately Important	Extremely Important

8. How many friends or family members also take part in this activity either with you or separately?

#_____

9 a. How many of those friends and family members taking part in this activity did you introduce to it?

#_____

b. How many introduced you?

#_____

This is a questionnaire to find out how people believe they will do in certain situations. Each item consists of a 5-point scale and a belief statement regarding one's expectations about events. Please indicate the degree to which you believe the statement would apply to you by writing the appropriate number (1-5) in the space to the left of each statement. Give the answer that you truly believe best applies to you and not what you would like to be true or what you think others would like to hear. Answer the items carefully, but do not spend too much time on any one item. Be sure to find an answer for every item, even if the statement describes a situation you do not presently expect to encounter. Answer as if you were going to be in each situation. Also try to respond to each item independently when making a choice; do not be influenced by your previous choices.

1 = Highly Improbable
2 = Moderately Improbable
3 = Neither Probable Nor Improbable
4 = Moderately Probable
5 = Highly Probable

In the future, I expect that I will:

_____ 1. be unable to accomplish my goals.

_____ 2. not be very good at learning new skills.

_____ 3. carry through my responsibilities successfully.

_____ 4. discover that the good in life outweighs the bad.

_____ 5. get the promotions I deserve.

_____ 6. succeed in the projects I undertake.

_____ 7. discover that my life is not getting much better.

_____ 8. be listened to when I speak.

_____ 9. succeed at most things I try.

_____10. be successful in my endeavors in the long run.

We are interested in your views on the nature of personal change. By personal change we mean changes which you deliberately choose, involving significant alterations in attitudes or behaviors. Place an "X" on the space on each line that best represents your estimate of the nature of significant change for you.

Significant change is:

Difficult   :___:___:___:___:___:___:___: Easy

Frequent   :___:___:___:___:___:___:___: Rare

Pleasant   :___:___:___:___:___:___:___: Unpleasant

Disruptive   :___:___:___:___:___:___:___: Stabilizing

Slow :   :___:___:___:___:___:___:___: Quick

Weak   :___:___:___:___:___:___:___: Strong

Permanent   :___:___:___:___:___:___:___: Temporary

Negative   :___:___:___:___:___:___:___: Positive

Real   :___:___:___:___:___:___:___: Illusory

Superficial   :___:___:___:___:___:___:___: Deep

Costly   :___:___:___:___:___:___:___: Beneficial

Good   :___:___:___:___:___:___:___: Bad

Painful   :___:___:___:___:___:___:___: Enjoyable

Please complete each of the following by circling the phrase closest to your opinion about the nature of change.

1. I believe change is:

0	1	2	3	4
Possible For None	Possible For Few	Possible For Some	Possible For Many	Possible For All

Indicate how much you agree with the statements below by circling one of the responses which follow.

2. Once significant change is achieved in one area, other changes are likely to follow with greater ease.

1	2	3	4	5
Strongly Agree	Moderately Agree	Neither Agree Nor Disagree	Moderately Agree	Strongly Agree

3. No matter how many times significant change is achieved, the next change is just as difficult.

1	2	3	4	5
Strongly Agree	Moderately Agree	Neither Agree Nor Disagree	Moderately Agree	Strongly Agree

4. Compared to others around my age, the significant personal changes I have been through in the past year were:

1	2	3
Fewer Than Most	About As Many As Most	More Than Most

5. Most of the changes I made in the past year were:

1	2	3	4	5
Extremely Desirable	Moderately Desirable	Neutral	Moderately Undesirable	Extremely Undesirable

6. People can make significant changes in:

4	3	2	1	0
Anything	Many Things	Some Things	Few Things	Nothing

Appendix B

AGREEMENT entered into this 6th day of May, 1985, between Jeffrey D. Fisher and Jack M. Chinsky (hereafter called the "Researchers"), the University of Connecticut, and Werner Erhard and Associates (hereafter called the "Forum Sponsor"). Any individual or organization who provides financial support for the research project described herein (hereafter called the "Project") will be referred to by the term "Research Sponsors." The phrase, "Network-sponsored events" refers to any current or subsequent events undertaken by the Forum Sponsor, including "Forums" and "Graduate Seminars".

The Researchers will undertake a program of research as the Project under the following terms and conditions:

1. *Nature of the research* - The research will consist of a series of studies designed to assess the social, psychological, and health-related effects of Network-sponsored events. The explicit goals of the research are: (a) to provide a broad investigation of the outcomes of the Forum; (b) to address certain problems of research methodology in the study of large group programs; and (c) to contribute to current work in clinical, social, and community psychology.

2. *Intention of the Forum Sponsor in Making the Forum Available for Study* - The Forum, an original method of inquiry applicable across a wide spectrum of human endeavor, is intended to contribute toward a greater understanding of human effectiveness and accomplishment. The intention of the Forum Sponsor in granting permission for this study is to make the work of the Forum available for research by the methods and analytical tools of other disciplines. The Forum Sponsor offers the Forum for study with a full comprehension of and commitment to the principles of academic freedom.

3. *Commitments of the Forum Sponsor* - the Forum Sponsor will arrange for the cost of the research to be paid to the University of Connecticut Division of Grants and Contracts. The costs will include: all salaries and fringe benefits (when fringe benefits are applicable); consultant costs, the costs of all materials, travel, communications, shipping, services, and equipment necessary for the Project; and any applicable charges for indirect costs in accordance with the University's customary accounting methods.

The Forum Sponsor agrees to arrange for all payments for costs related to expenses in the following manner. Once a particular "phase" of the research has been agreed to by Forum Sponsor and Researchers, the Forum Sponsor will arrange for sufficient funds to cover the expenses of that "phase" to be sent to the Researchers before the actual implementation of such a "phase" begins.

The cost of phase I - piloting experimental procedures and developing a full proposal for subsequent research is $88,000. This must be deposited with the University of Connecticut Division of Grants and Contracts before May 15, 1985, when pilot research is scheduled to begin.

The Forum Sponsor also agrees to the following:

a) That the Forum Sponsor will not attempt to dictate the design of the study and the composition of the Research Team in any way.

b) That the Forum Sponsor will not impede the Researchers' access to subjects who will include participants in current Network-sponsored events and control groups which will be defined by the Researchers.

c) That the Forum Sponsor agrees not to institute any legal action or attempt to hold Researchers or the University of Connecticut liable for any results of the study or the subsequent publication of results which they might view as unfavorable or from any negative effects which may accrue to the Forum Sponsor as a result of the research or its publication.

d) That the Forum Sponsor yields to the Researchers' ownership and disposition of all data and any research materials purchased with Research Sponsors' funds.

e) That the Forum Sponsor assumes full liability and agrees to hold the Researchers and the University of Connecticut harmless for any claims made against the Researchers or the Research Team by or on behalf of persons who participate in Network-sponsored events which the Researchers include as part of the Project, or by any third party, provided such claims do not involve the direct effects of testing or of any other actual work performed by the Researchers or the Research Team in any phase of the Project.

f) That the Forum Sponsor waives the right to approve any of the research procedures to be used by the Researchers, except for procedures which are reasonably deemed by the Forum Sponsor to interfere with the successful delivery of the Network-sponsored event under consideration.

g) That the Forum Sponsor waives the right to approve the research instruments employed by the Researchers, provided these instruments have been approved by the Human Experimentation Committee to whom the Researchers account.

h) That the Forum Sponsor may request but will not require the Researchers to provide an account of any findings of the research before the end of the Project. Both the Forum Sponsor and the Research Sponsors may require progress reports, i.e., accounts of how much of the research has been completed by a particular point in time.

4. *Commitments of Researchers* - The research will be conducted under the supervision of Jeffrey D. Fisher and Jack M. Chinsky. The cost of each phase of the research will be established in a mutually agreed upon budget which the Researchers will not exceed without specific written authorization from the Forum Sponsor.

The Researchers also agree to the following:

a) That the Researchers will present the results in an impartial, scholarly manner.

b) That the Researchers will consult with the Forum Sponsor when they deem that it would be useful to insure a fair assessment.

c) Any claims of negligence entered by anyone against the Researchers, the Research Team, or the University of Connecticut shall be brought in accordance with Chapter 53 of the Connecticut General Statutes.

d) That the Researchers (1) will, to the extent permissible under the laws of the State of Connecticut, protect and maintain the confidentiality of the names and identities of the participants in Network-sponsored events which the Researchers study or observe, as well as the statements made or actions taken by such participants during the course of Network-sponsored events; and (2) will not violate the copyright of Werner Erhard or Werner Erhard and Associates in and to the substantive content of the material delivered in Network-sponsored events. By "not violate the copyright" is meant (i) that the Researchers will not reprint, publish, copy, disseminate or show to any unauthorized party, any printed, written, audiorecorded, or videorecorded material which is the property of Werner Erhard and Associates without the express written permission of Werner Erhard or his designee, (ii) that neither the Researchers nor any employees of the Research Institutions shall use any such material or any of the concepts contained therein for commercial use or resale without the express written permission of Werner Erhard or his designee. In no case shall permission to use such material for legitimate scholarly purposes be unreasonably withheld. This agreement is applicable to the Researchers; the Research Team; any person who is engaged by the Researchers to perform any portion of the work in connection with the Project; and any other person connected with the research, the Research Team, or the University of Connecticut.

e) The Researchers are free to describe any aspect of the Forum or other network-sponsored events in scholarly discussions, presentations, published manuscripts, or books. These descriptions may include verbatim accounts necessary for accurate description to a scientific audience. In no case will this be considered a copyright violation by the Forum Sponsor, nor shall it require that permission be granted.

5. *Sponsor's Use of Research* - (a) Prior to publication, neither the Forum Sponsor nor the Research Sponsors may use the names or institutions of the Researchers or refer to the results of the research in news releases, publicity, advertising, or product promotion without prior written approval of the Researchers and the University of Connecticut Vice President of Graduate Education and Research, which approval will not be unreasonably withheld. Werner Erhard and Associates will not have the right to use the name of any researcher or institution associated with the project on any material disseminated by the Network for the above purposes without prior consent of the researcher and the University of Connecticut. Any results published by the Forum Sponsor or quoted by the Forum Sponsor for publication will be presented with sufficient context drawn from the results of the Research as a whole to prevent misrepresentation or distortion. For this purpose, "sufficient context" will be determined by the Researchers or their representatives, which determination will not be unreasonably made.

(b) Sponsor's use of research following publication. The results of the research following their publication in professional journals and other outlets in which professionals publish their results become part of the public domain, and anyone citing those results is subject to the laws and guidelines which govern the use of published material. After publication, the fact of the research and the fact of the Researchers having conducted the research will be public knowledge, and the Forum Sponsor is free to represent that fact in the normal course of business. It is understood that the Forum Sponsor in the course of business is frequently requested to provide access to studies performed on the Forum, and this agreement is in no way intended to limit the Forum Sponsor from making known, in response to an inquiry, the fact of the existence of the research or its results as published by the authors. However, the Forum Sponsor agrees, even after publication, not to represent the results of the research as an endorsement of the Forum or any aspect of it by either the Researchers or the University of Connecticut unless an endorsement is specifically stated as such in published material.

This agreement is taken to mean that the Forum Sponsor will not, even after publication, use the names of the Researchers nor of the University of Connecticut in product promotion, advertisement, publicity or the like without the prior written approval of the Researchers and the University of Connecticut Vice President of Graduate Education and Research. The Forum Sponsor may, however, inform people of the fact of the research, refer people to it, include references to it in bibliographic references, and the like. In short, the Forum Sponsor will not be restricted from representing the results of the research and the fact of the research in any non-promotional manner.

6. *Publication and dissemination by Researchers* - University research activities are conduced as an integral part of the educational program and are intended to contribute to the advancement of knowledge. Research forms the basis for books, articles in professional journals, seminar reports, and presentations at professional society meetings. In addition, theses and dissertation work performed by graduate students on research projects must be publishable if they are to receive degree credit. The Researchers cannot therefore undertake research or studies, the results of which cannot be published without the Sponsor's prior approval.

Similarly, such publications, reports, and theses reflect the professional judgement and conclusions reached by the Research Team. The Sponsors may not require that such written and oral presentations be modified, except as they may incidentally misrepresent non-scientific facts relating to the Forum Sponsor's history, policies, business practices, and network structure. (Nonscientific facts shall be understood to be those facts that are neither related to independent or dependent measures under discussion.) Therefore, the Researchers will be free to present and/or publish the results of the research. The Sponsors will be provided with a copy prior to the date of publication and following any presentation.

In addition, the Researchers will have the right to publish and discuss results at any time during the course of the research. Notwithstanding the foregoing, the Researchers and Research Team will not publish or disseminate in written or oral form any information which is part of this research if such publication or dissemination will violate the agreements regarding confidentiality and non-violation of copyright as provided in Article 4, above.

7. *Assignment* - Neither party may assign any or all of its rights or obligations under this Agreement without the prior written consent of the other party.

8. *Notices* - Any notice, request, approval, consent, or payment under this

Agreement (collectively "Notice") shall be in writing, and if not hand-delivered, shall be mailed by certified mail, return receipt requested, and be addressed to the Researchers, the Sponsors, or their designees, as follows:

With respect to the Researchers:
Jeffrey D. Fisher, Ph.D.
Department of Psychology
University of Connecticut
U-20, Room 107, 406 Cross Campus Road
Storrs, CT 06268

Jack M. Chinsky
Department of Psychology
University of Connecticut
U-30, Room 107, 406 Cross Campus Road
Storrs, CT 06268

With respect to the administration of the contract and payments:
Richard C. Carterud
Director, Office of Grants and Contracts
Box U-151, Room 114
28 Mansfield Road
University of Connecticut
Storrs, CT 06268

With respect to the Sponsors:
Dr. John J. Mantos
Executive Director
Division of Research and Programs
Werner Erhard and Associates
765 California Street
San Francisco, CA 94108

Notice shall be effective when received.

9. *Term of the Agreement* - The following elements in the Agreement will remain in force for the duration of any phases of research, the performance of which have been mutually agreed to by the Forum Sponsor and the Researchers: 1,2,3,3a,3b,3f,3g,3h,4,4b.

The following elements of the agreement will survive in perpetuity: 3c, 3d, 3e, 4a, 4c, 4d, 4e, 5a, 6, 7, and 8.

10. *Termination* - Research being conducted under this agreement may be terminated by either party at any time upon giving the other party sixty (60) days prior written notice. Upon the giving of such notice of termination, both parties will proceed in an orderly fashion to terminate any outstanding commitments and to conclude the work. Upon termination, the Researchers will be reimbursed for all costs and non-cancellable commitments incurred in the performance of the Research prior to the notice of termination which have not been reimbursed to the Researchers; provided that such reimbursement will not exceed the total estimated cost of the Project as Provided in Article 3, above. If any students are supported under this Agreement, the Forum Sponsor will remain liable for the full costs of such students through the end of the academic year. If the agreement is terminated after March 15th of an academic year, the Forum Sponsor will be liable for the full costs of such students through the end of the following academic year, even if such costs exceed the total estimated cost of the project, as provided in Article 3.

In the event of termination, the Researchers will prepare a final report of all costs incurred and all funds received within ninety (90) days of the effective date of termination. The Researchers will send one (1) copy of the report to the Forum Sponsor and agree to return any excess funds advanced over costs incurred. If any costs are due to the Researchers, such costs will then be paid forthwith.

In the event of termination, the Researchers will review the data collected to that point an inform the Forum Sponsor of whatever findings have been produced to that point and which the Researchers consider relevant to the Forum Sponsor or which the Researchers consider should be known by the Forum Sponsor. The Forum Sponsor may request but may not require copies of any data produced. What, if any, data is to be turned over to the Forum Sponsor in the event of termination will be determined solely by the researchers.

11. All claims arising from any act, omission, or negligence against the University of Connecticut or its employees arising out of this Agreement, or any breach thereof, shall be filed as a claim against the State of Connecticut in accordance with Chapter 53 of the Connecticut General Statutes.

12. *Binding Nature of Agreement* - This Agreement shall be binding upon and inure to the parties hereto, their heirs, executors, administrators, trustees, representatives, successors, and assigns.

IN WITNESS WHEREOF, the parties have caused this Agreement to be executed as of the day an year first written above.